How to Pass

SECOND EDITION

NATIONAL 5

French

Douglas Angus

HODDER
GIBSON
AN HACHETTE UK COMPANY

Audio files for the Listening tasks in this book are available online. Visit www.hoddergibson.co.uk and click on 'Updates & extras'.

The Publishers would like to thank the following for permission to reproduce copyright material:

Acknowledgements

p.viii Contexts, topics and topic development table is from National 5 Modern Languages Course Support Notes, https://www.sqa.org.uk/files_ccc/ModernLanguagesCourseSpecN5.pdf copyright © Scottish Qualifications Authority; **pp.3–4** 'Bien se préparer à un examen' is based on an article that appeared on www.phosphore.com; **pp.5–6** 'Il n'est pas simple de trouver une place dans le monde de la coiffure aujourd'hui' is from an article that appeared on www.phosphore.com; **pp.11–12** film reviews are adapted from reviews of *Entre les murs* at www.Amazon.fr; **pp.22–3** 'Trouver son premier emploi n'est jamais simple' and questions are from National 5 French Reading Specimen Paper, https://www.sqa.org.uk/files_ccc/FrenchReadingSQPN5.pdf copyright © Scottish Qualifications Authority; **pp.24–5** 'À minuit, au lit!' and questions are from Standard Grade French 2001 / Credit Reading Specimen Question Paper Question 1, copyright © Scottish Qualifications Authority; **pp.31–3** 'Les stages à l'étranger' is from an article that appeared on www.phosphore.com; **pp.60–1** National 5 French Talking General Marking Instructions are from Modern Languages Performance: Talking General assessment information, https://www.sqa.org.uk/files_ccc/ModernLanguagesCourseSpecN5.pdf copyright © Scottish Qualifications Authority; **p.63** National 5 French Specimen Paper Writing task, https://www.sqa.org.uk/files_ccc/FrenchWritingSQPN5.pdf copyright © Scottish Qualifications Authority; **pp.66–7** National 5 French Grade Categories for Writing table is from National 5 French Specimen Paper, https://www.sqa.org.uk/files_ccc/FrenchWritingSQPN5.pdf copyright © Scottish Qualifications Authority; **pp.69–70** Marking Instruction for Writing is from National 5 French Course Specification, https://www.sqa.org.uk/files_ccc/ModernLanguagesCourseSpecN5.pdf copyright © Scottish Qualifications Authority.

Audio engineering: Phil Booth, Heriot-Watt University, Edinburgh.

Every effort has been made to trace all copyright holders, but if any have been inadvertently overlooked the Publishers will be pleased to make the necessary arrangements at the first opportunity.

Although every effort has been made to ensure that website addresses are correct at time of going to press, Hodder Gibson cannot be held responsible for the content of any website mentioned in this book. It is sometimes possible to find a relocated web page by typing in the address of the home page for a website in the URL window of your browser.

Hachette UK's policy is to use papers that are natural, renewable and recyclable products and made from wood grown in sustainable forests. The logging and manufacturing processes are expected to conform to the environmental regulations of the country of origin.

Orders: please contact Bookpoint Ltd, 130 Park Drive, Milton Park, Abingdon, Oxon OX14 4SE. Telephone: (44) 01235 827720. Fax: (44) 01235 400454. Lines are open 9.00–5.00, Monday to Saturday, with a 24-hour message answering service. Visit our website at www.hoddereducation.co.uk. Hodder Gibson can also be contacted directly at hoddergibson@hodder.co.uk

© Douglas Angus 2018

First published in 2018 by
Hodder Gibson, an imprint of Hodder Education,
An Hachette UK Company
211 St Vincent Street
Glasgow G2 5QY

Impression number	5	4	3	2	1
Year		2022 2021 2020 2019 2018			

Cover photo © Juergen Faelchle/Shutterstock.com
Illustrations by Emma Golley at Redmoor Design
Typeset in 13/15 Cronos Pro (Light) by Aptara, Inc.
Printed in India
A catalogue record for this title is available from the British Library
ISBN: 978 1 510 42090 8

Contents

Introduction   iv

Chapter 1 How to tackle reading and listening   1

Chapter 2 Answers and transcripts for reading and listening tasks   9

Chapter 3 How to tackle talking and writing   13

Chapter 4 Reading at National 5   21

Chapter 5 Answers for reading tasks   37

Chapter 6 Listening at National 5   39

Chapter 7 Transcripts and answers for listening tasks   45

Chapter 8 Talking: Preparing for the assessment   51

Chapter 9 Writing: The final exam   62

Chapter 10 Writing: The assignment   68

Chapter 11 Structures and opinions   74

Chapter 12 Vocabulary   78

Introduction

What is the course like?

National 5 French will test you on four skills: reading, listening, talking and writing. All of these skills will be taught over the course of your studies by your teacher to help you pass the final exam. Three of the skills – reading, listening and writing – will be assessed at the end of the course in an external exam, set and marked by SQA, which will provide you with a grade A, B, C or D. In addition, at some point in the year, you will complete a writing assignment which will also be marked by SQA , and carry out a talking assessment which will be marked by your teacher.

In this book you will find chapters to help you work on and revise each skill. The language you will need relates to four contexts: **society**, **learning**, **employability** and **culture**. On page viii you will find a list of possible topic areas within these contexts which you could expect at National 5.

How is my final scaled mark made up?

You will be given a mark for each of the four skills. A potential 120 marks, on which your final grade will be based, are divided up as follows after scaling:
- Reading: 30 marks
- Listening: 30 marks
- Talking: 30 marks
- Writing: 30 (15 exam/15 assignment) marks.

This will then be converted into a mark out of 100, making each skill worth 25% of your total.

What do I have to know?

You will need to know basic vocabulary covering a list of topic areas, which you will find in the table on page viii. This will help you listen to and read French more easily, and will also help you produce your own written and spoken French. You will find lists of useful vocabulary with many of the talking and writing preparation tasks, as well as with the listening tasks. Chapter 12 'Vocabulary' will also be useful.

You will need to know the basics of grammar, so that you can write and speak French correctly. This is something you will work on as you go through the course. Some guidelines are given later in this chapter. You will also find some guidance in Chapter 11 'Structures and opinions'. There is further work on producing your own French in Chapter 8 'Talking' and Chapters 9 and 10 'Writing'.

You must be able to use a dictionary to help you understand French in the reading exam, and to find words you need for your talking and writing. You should also use your dictionary to check your verb endings.

What exactly is involved in the exam?

Reading

Reading will be assessed by an external exam. There will be one paper that will include three separate texts, each of up to 200 words. Questions will be set and answered in English. Unusual words may be translated for you in a glossary.

You will be allowed to use a French dictionary.

Writing

Writing will be assessed by one piece of work that you will produce after you have done the reading. You will be expected to respond to a stimulus with six bullet points, all of which you must address. The contexts for the writing will be a combination of **society**, **learning**, **employability** and **culture**.

The reading and writing paper will last 1 hour 30 minutes.

You will also write an assignment of 120–200 words under controlled conditions. See Chapter 10 'Writing: The assignment' for details.

Listening

Listening will be assessed by an external exam. There will be two separate parts, one a presentation or monologue, the other a conversation or dialogue. You will hear the French three times, and the whole assessment will last up to 30 minutes.

Questions will be set and answered in English.

You will *not* be allowed to use a French–English dictionary.

The reading, listening and writing tests will be marked externally by SQA.

Talking

Talking will be assessed by your teacher and externally moderated by SQA.

You will be expected to carry out a spoken presentation and conversation in French from one of the following contexts: **society**, **learning**, **employability**, **culture**. You will agree which one with your teacher. You will also agree with your teacher when your assessment will take place. The presentation will be worth 10 marks and the conversation 20 marks.

Basic grammar

When marking your work, teachers will be looking for accuracy in basic structures. This is straightforward, simple language, and you should be able to show you can do everything listed in the box on the next page.

What you should know

Verbs

★ Use the correct form of the verb. This includes using subject pronouns (like *je, il, elle*) and correct verb endings, matching the subject.
★ Use *ne … pas, ne … jamais*, etc.
★ Ask simple questions correctly.
★ Use 'modal' verbs, such as *vouloir* and *pouvoir*, and the auxiliary verbs *avoir* and *être*.
★ Use verbs fairly accurately in 'personal' language and 'polite' language. This includes the correct polite verb forms for requests (*voulez-vous …, je voudrais …*) and also the correct verb forms for plural subjects: *mes sœurs ont …, mes amis sont …*
★ Use present, future, imperfect, perfect and conditional tenses.

Nouns

★ Use the correct type of article/determiner (*un/une/des, le/la/les, ce/cette/ces*) and, if you can, the correct form (for example, correct gender or number).
★ Use nouns with the correct gender form of article and adjective.
★ Use the words for 'my' and 'your' correctly.

Pronouns

★ Use the correct form of subject or object pronouns, and put them in the correct place.

Prepositions

★ Use the correct preposition, and know what it does to articles and pronouns (*à* and *le = au, pour* and *je = pour moi*).

For better grades, you will have to do more than this. The language resource column in the table on pages 69–70 in Chapter 10 shows what examiners are going to be looking for. When you are working through the talking and writing chapters, it will be useful to refer to these pages sometimes so that you can show off your knowledge of French to the examiner!

How do I go about learning vocabulary?

The best way to revise is to practise. Although different people have different ways of learning vocabulary, the following ways might be useful to you.

Hints & tips ★

✓ Try writing out a list of words, then reading them out. Cover up the French words, and see if you can remember the words in English, and of course the other way round.

✓ Read things over several times on different occasions.

✓ Check your memorising by either covering one part and remembering the other, or by asking someone to do it with you (a friend or parent). If you have someone to help you, ask them to say a word in English, which you have to put into French.

✓ Try to get your words organised into areas, so they all hang together and make sense to you.

✓ Use spidergrams of related words.

What kind of vocabulary will I need to know?

On the next page you will find the topic areas that you are likely to be studying as part of your course. You will also find vocabulary lists in Chapter 12 to help you prepare for assessments and to revise.

Contexts, topics and topic development you can expect at National 5

Society	Family and friends	Getting on with family members/who have influenced you in your life ● Having arguments ● Ideal parents ● Different types of friends ● Peer pressure
	Lifestyles	● Lifestyle-related illnesses ● Advantages and disadvantages of healthy/unhealthy lifestyle
	Media	● Impact of TV reality shows ● Advantages/disadvantages of new technology, e.g. internet, mobile phones
	Global languages	● Language learning and relevance
	Citizenship	● Description of local area as a tourist centre ● Comparison of town and country life ● Being environmentally friendly in the home
Learning	Learning in context	● Talk about what learning activities you like/dislike in modern languages/in each subject ● Preparing for exams
	Education	● Comparing education systems ● Improving own education system ● Learner responsibilities
Employability	Jobs	● Part-time jobs and studying ● Qualities for present/future jobs, future plans
	Work and CVs	● Planning, reporting back on work experience ● Reviewing achievements/ambitions
Culture	Planning a trip	● Importance of travel and learning a foreign language ● Describing your best holiday/trip, attitudes to travel
	Other countries	● Aspects of other countries including educational, social, historical, political aspects
	Celebrating a special event	● Comparing special occasions/traditions/celebrations/events in another country ● Importance of customs/traditions
	Literature of another country	● Literary fiction, e.g. short stories – understanding and analysis
	Film and television	● Studying films in the modern language ● Studying television in other countries

How to tackle reading and listening

Reading

Reading is a skill which you should develop, as it will make it easier for you in the final exam. It is worth looking at your use of the dictionary, developing guessing skills and seeing how different forms of questions look. It is also worth looking carefully at marking schemes to see the kind of answers that are acceptable. Remember that usually you will be expected to answer with more than one word and to give details. Get used to looking at the number of marks attached to each question to see how long the answer might be. The following reading tasks should help you develop your skills. You will find more guidance on reading skills in Chapter 4 'Reading at National 5'.

Here are four possible tasks, one from each context, which you can try. The answers are in the next chapter.

Society: Citizenship

For this task, you have to answer questions and fill out a true/false choice box.

You read the article below about how to deal with hedgehogs in your garden.

C'est l'automne et je vois un jeune hérisson dans mon jardin.

Qu'est-ce que je dois faire?

Avant l'hiver, le hérisson cherche à économiser autant de calories que possible. Quand il fait trop froid et que la nourriture devient trop difficile à trouver, il entre en hibernation dans un nid bien isolé. Mais pendant tout l'automne, il mange comme quatre pour accumuler un maximum de réserves de graisse.

Ainsi, un jeune hérisson, pour avoir de bonnes chances de survivre, doit atteindre un poids de 450 g avant de commencer son hibernation.

Si tu trouves un jeune hérisson encore actif à l'automne, tu peux donc lui offrir de la nourriture et un bon nid bien isolé.

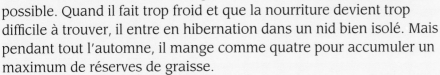

Questions ❓

1   What two reasons are given for hedgehogs going into hibernation? **2**

....

....

2   What two pieces of advice are you given if you find a hedgehog? **2**

....

....

You read the rest of the article, which gives you advice on what kinds of food you should give a hedgehog.

Quels aliments?

Le mieux est de mettre dans une assiette ou un bol:

● de la nourriture pour chaton (ou pour chat)
● comme pour un chat, des restes de nourriture (mais pas trop salés)
● des petits yaourts (les offrir au hérisson dans leur petit pot de plastique, en enlevant simplement le carré de papier alu qui les ferme – cela empêche les chats de les manger, mais permet aux jeunes hérissons de manger le petit yaourt, avec leur *museau pointu).

museau – muzzle

Question ❓

3   Are the following statements **true** or **false**? Write T or F in the boxes below. **4**

You should put out food on a plate.	
You should keep the cat away.	
You should never put out table scraps.	
You should put out yoghurts in their pots.	

Question ❓

4   Who do you think this article was aimed at? Give a reason for your answer. **1**

....

....

Learning: Preparing for exams

For this task, we have provided two possible ways for you to demonstrate understanding. There is a set of questions of the type that will be in the final exam, with a set of answers for you to check how well you have done. Alternatively, you could try using the text to help you prepare for either the talking or the writing assignment you will have to carry out at one point. That means using the text as the basis for a piece of talking or writing in French that gives your own thoughts on preparing for an exam.

The following text gives advice to young French people on how to prepare for 'D-Day': the day of an important exam! The text talks about the importance of the 'four Rs'.

Bien se préparer à un examen
Jusqu'au jour J

Pour bien réussir un examen, il est important d'arriver le jour J dans les meilleures conditions. Pour cela, une règle est très utile: la règle des « 4R ».

Révise
Quinze jours avant l'examen, tu dois organiser tout ton matériel! Révise à l'aide des livres, des formules, de tes carnets de vocabulaire. Va à l'essentiel: il est important de ne pas te perdre dans des détails superflus!

Relis
Relis toutes les copies que ton professeur a corrigées pendant l'année.

Régularise-toi
Essaie de ne pas te coucher tard (ne perturbe pas ton biorythme), ne mange pas trop, et évite le stress et les efforts sportifs épuisants. Et il ne faut pas prendre des médicaments dopants ou calmants. ⇨

Repose-toi

Dors suffisamment. Oxygène-toi: vas te promener au grand air.

La veille de l'examen, prépare ton matériel (stylos, gomme, crayon, compas, calculette et dictionnaire s'ils sont autorisés, ciseaux, colle, buvard, montre) et ta carte d'identité.

Couche-toi tôt, après avoir réglé deux réveils (pour le cas où l'un serait défaillant!).

Le jour J

Le matin de l'examen: mange un petit-déjeuner nourrissant, même si tu n'as pas faim. Arrive au centre d'examen légèrement en avance.

Organise ton temps d'épreuve. Lis plusieurs fois chaque question. Fixe-toi rapidement un budget temps pour les différentes étapes de ton travail.

Après, relis ta copie, fais attention à l'orthographe, à la ponctuation, aux accents et à la présentation en général.

Questions ?

1 The first 'R' is Revise.
   a) When should you start this according to the text? **1**
   ....
   b) What might you use to help you? **2**
   ....

2 The second 'R' is Reread.
   What does the article tell you to read again? **2**
   ....

3 The fourth 'R' is Rest.
   a) State the two things you should organise the night before. **2**
   ....
   ....
   b) What are the final two pieces of advice for the night before? **2**
   ....

4 The final part of the text is about the day of the exam itself.
   a) What should you do before the exam? **1**
   ....
   b) What should you do with each question? **1**
   ....
   c) State any two things you should look at, at the end of the exam. **2**
   ....
   ....

5 Overall, the author gives a number of pieces of advice relating to health. Can you summarise these? **6**
   ....
   ....
   ....

Preparing a talking or writing assignment

Read the advice given in the text again, and write in English the five pieces of advice you think are most useful. Then make up a PowerPoint presentation *in French* giving **your** advice on how best to prepare for an exam. This should include at least six slides with pieces of advice. You should prepare a talk to accompany it and be ready to answer questions on your presentation. Alternatively, choose the five pieces of advice you think are most useful, make a brief note of them in English, then write 20–30 words in French on each one with your own ideas.

Employability

In this task, you are asked not to answer questions, but to summarise the disadvantages that someone thinking about taking up hairdressing as a profession should consider. Your answer can be bullet points or a short paragraph. Again, you can use this to help you prepare for either a talking or a writing assignment. Although the text is quite long, you should skim through, not using a dictionary all the time, and highlight where you think the answers are. Then look at those areas in greater detail.

Read the article below about hairdressing as an occupation. Find five potential disadvantages for young people who take up this career.

Coiffeur

Il n'est pas simple de trouver une place dans le monde de la coiffure aujourd'hui.

De nombreux apprentis ne trouvent pas d'emploi après l'obtention de leur diplôme. Et le secteur est marqué par de toutes petites structures: leur taille moyenne est de 2,9 personnes par salon. La profession est encore très dominée par les femmes: seuls 15% des coiffeurs sont des hommes. Mais les employeurs assurent qu'un bon coiffeur jeune trouvera un emploi, s'il est doué … ⇨

Que fait-il?

La majorité des coiffeurs travaillent en salon de coiffure. Le rôle de ce salarié consiste à accueillir les clients, les écouter et les conseiller sur la coupe choisie. Il procède alors au shampoing, à la coupe et éventuellement à d'autres soins: coloration, brushing, etc.

Le métier de coiffeur implique de longs moments en position debout, à piétiner, dans des postures fatigantes pour les bras, le dos et les jambes. Mieux vaut être résistant physiquement. Il est également déconseillé aux jeunes ayant un terrain allergique de se lancer dans le secteur car l'utilisation de produits parfois toxiques et les ambiances humides et chaudes pourraient être très gênantes. Les horaires sont assez irréguliers et normalement on travaille le samedi.

Où travaille-t-il?

La majorité manie les ciseaux dans un salon de coiffure, de taille variable. Les autres travaillent dans un studio de mode, ou dans des loges de théâtre et de cinéma. Certains, de plus en plus nombreux, exercent leur profession directement au domicile de leur client.

Ses qualités

- Habilité manuelle
- Sens et goût artistique
- Bon contact humain

Salaire et formation

Un coiffeur salarié gagne environ 1 200 euros nets par mois. La formation dure en général deux ans, mais peut être réduite à un an pour les titulaires du bac ou, au contraire, rallongée d'un an pour les jeunes en apprentissage.

Culture: Other countries

For this task, you are asked to translate key facts quite accurately, sticking closely to the original. It is a shorter text, but you will have to give all the details asked for. It is a guided translation.

Des chiffres-clés sur la planète

1	Une personne sur cinq vit avec moins d'un dollar par jour.
2	25% de la population mondiale vit sans électricité.
3	Les glaciers de l'Himalaya pourraient disparaître d'ici à 2035.
4	815 millions de personnes sont sous-alimentées.
5	10% de la population mondiale possède 80% des richesses.
6	20% de la population mondiale n'a pas accès à l'eau potable.
7	Toutes les deux secondes, une forêt de la taille d'un terrain de football disparaît.

Questions ?

Complete the following sentences.

1 One person in ....
2 25% of the world's population lives ....
3 Himalayan glaciers .... by 2035.
4 815 million people ....
5 10% of the world's ....
6 20% of the world's ....
7 Every two seconds .... disappears.

Why has the author chosen these facts to highlight?

Listening

Listening is another skill that improves above all with practice. So, take every opportunity you can to practise listening. Take your time with the following tasks, replay them as often as you want and get used to listening to and understanding the French. When you have tried the tasks, listen again with the transcript in front of you to see the connections between the written and the spoken word.

Society: Advantages and disadvantages of mobile phones

For this task, you will hear two people talking about what mobile phones mean to them. You should make a note of the key points each speaker makes for and against mobile phones, then summarise these key points *in English*. You should find at least six positives and two negatives.

Learning: Learner responsibilities

For this task, you will hear an excerpt from a radio programme in which a young French person looks for help, as he can't seem to remember what he has studied for his homework. Listen to it, and select three pieces of advice you think are important. Write them down *in English*.

éloigner	*to take/move away*
la veille	*the evening before*
le cerveau	*the brain*

Employability: A job interview

This task needs two people as it is a conversation. It could be you and a teacher, or you and another student. Understanding what someone is saying and reporting on it in English is a key skill. This task can also help you prepare for the discussion part of the talking assessment you will be carrying out with your teacher.

The context is applying for a work experience placement (*un stage*) in France. One person will take on the role of the interviewer, the other the role of the applicant. If you are taking on the role of the interviewer, you will have to make a note of the applicant's responses and report back on them *in English*. If you are the applicant, understanding the questions and answering them in an appropriate fashion is the kind of practice that is invaluable. Just make sure the questions are not asked in a set order so that it is obvious you have not learned the answers in a specific order – you need to be able to demonstrate you have actually understood the question. Remember to start and finish with the normal greeting and leave-taking phrases, and to use *vous*. Here is a list of some of the questions you might use.

- *Comment vous appelez-vous?*
- *Depuis combien de temps apprenez-vous le français?*
- *Pourquoi voulez-vous faire ce stage?*
- *Est-ce que vous avez déjà fait un stage en Écosse?*
- *Vous avez de l'expérience d'un travail comme celui-ci?*
- *Quels sont vos intérêts?*
- *Quels sont vos points forts?* (strengths)
- *Et quels sont vos points forts en informatique?*

Culture: Films in the foreign language

For this activity, you will hear two different reviews of a French film, *Entre les murs*, about a teacher's experiences in a tough school just outside Paris. The film was based on a novel, which in turn was based on the author's (Bégaudeau's) own experiences as a teacher.

One reviewer is positive, one not so. Listen to what they have to say, then give two or three contrasting views from each reviewer. This can be as bullet points or a short paragraph. Write your answer *in English*.

plus élevée – higher, more extreme

Reading answers

Society: Citizenship

1 it is too cold; food is too hard to find
2 give it food; and a well-insulated nest
3

You should put out food on a plate.	T
You should keep the cat away.	F
You should never put out table scraps.	F
You should put out yoghurts in their pots.	T

4 children or young people; the article addresses the reader as *tu*.

Learning: Preparing for exams

1 **a)** two weeks before the exam
  b) books; formulae; vocabulary notebooks (any two)
2 every test your teacher has marked over the year
3 **a)** the equipment you need; your identity card
  b) go to bed early; set two alarm clocks
4 **a)** have a good breakfast or get there slightly early
  b) read it several times
  c) spelling; punctuation; accents; presentation (any two)
5 **food:** eat a good breakfast on the day, don't eat too much
  sleep: don't go to bed too late, don't upset your biorhythm, go to bed early the night before the exam
  tiredness: don't get stressed, avoid exhausting sports, get fresh air
  medicine: don't take tranquilising medicines (any six pieces of advice)

Employability

- Many apprentices can't find a job when they finish.
- Only 15% are male.
- You spend a lot of time on your feet.
- It is tiring for legs, back and arms.
- The products used can be harmful to people with allergies.
- Humid and hot environments can be a challenge.
- The hours are irregular.
- Normally you have to work on Saturdays.
- Salary is about 1,200 euros a month. (any five)

Culture: Other countries

1 One person in **five lives on less than a dollar a day**.
2 25% of the world's population **lives without electricity**.
3 Himalayan glaciers **could/might disappear by 2035**.
4 815 million people **are undernourished.**
5 10% of the world's **population own 80% of its riches**.
6 20% of the world's **population doesn't have access to drinking water**.
7 Every two seconds, a **forest the size of a football pitch disappears**.

The author has chosen these facts because they are key points about the environment and/or problems in the less developed world.

Listening transcripts and answers
Society: Advantages and disadvantages of mobile phones

Raphaël

Chez nous, tout le monde a son portable, moi, mes parents et ma sœur qui a 10 ans. Depuis que j'en ai un, j'ai acquis de nombreuses libertés: je peux aller seul en ville, j'ai la permission de minuit dans les soirées. Mais au début, l'usage du portable n'était pas si simple. C'était surtout très cher, et souvent je n'avais plus d'argent dans mon portable. Mais maintenant je gère mes dépenses avec mon argent de poche, et la plupart du temps j'envoie des textos, ce qui est beaucoup moins cher. Alors, après quelque temps, je trouve ça génial. Je peux téléphoner à n'importe quelle heure, je peux être appelé même la nuit, sans réveiller les parents; enfin, je peux être sûr que mes messages ne seront pas écoutés, parce qu'ils ne sont pas sur le téléphone familial.

La mère

Je suis bien contente que mes enfants possèdent un portable à eux. Depuis qu'ils ont un portable, ça a libéré ma ligne de téléphone à la maison. Je me sens aussi sécurisée de savoir qu'ils peuvent appeler en cas d'urgence. Enfin, j'apprécie de ne plus avoir à me bagarrer pour les factures de téléphone. C'est à eux de payer leur portable de leur argent de poche. Je peux les appeler à n'importe quel endroit et à n'importe quelle heure si j'ai décidé à la dernière minute de changer de plan. Je dirais que pour moi, le seul problème, c'est qu'ils veulent régulièrement changer de portable pour le modèle le plus avancé.

Positives

- lots of freedom
- can go into town alone
- can go out till midnight
- texts are cheaper
- can call at any time, even at night
- nobody can hear what Raphaël is saying
- frees up the landline in the house
- can call home in an emergency
- no more fights about phone bill
- children pay for the phone from pocket money
- mother can call them if she has to change plans
  (any six)

Negatives

- can be expensive
- can run out of money on phone
- children regularly want to upgrade their phone
  (any two)

Learning: Learner responsibilities

Student: *Je travaille le soir pendant des heures mais à la fin, je m'aperçois que je n'ai rien retenu et cela me pose problème.*

Advice: *Vous avez un problème de méthode de travail. La première chose que vous devez faire, c'est éloigner tout ce qui peut perturber votre travail: jeux vidéo, Facebook, musique ... Ensuite, vous devez vous organiser: évaluer le travail que vous avez à faire en début de chaque semaine dans chaque matière. Chaque matin, ou la veille pour le lendemain, vous devez lister toutes les tâches et activités pour la journée, des plus petites aux plus importantes. Vous devez organiser et visualiser votre journée, alors votre cerveau s'y prépare déjà, il se programme. Vous savez où vous allez, ce qui vous donne davantage confiance en vous et peut vous motiver.*

Advice

- Get rid of things that might distract you, like Facebook, videos, music.
- Organise yourself at the start of each week, so you know what you have to do.
- Each morning, or the evening before, list what you have to do that day, little things as well as important ones.
- Organise and visualise your days to programme your brain.
- Know what you are going to do, to get more confidence and motivation. (any three)

Culture: Films in the foreign language

First reviewer

Qu'est-ce qu'on peut faire quand on est un mauvais prof? Écrire un mauvais livre pour raconter qu'on est un mauvais prof, mais que ce n'est pas entièrement sa faute, c'est le système. Et puis faire une mauvaise adaptation pour le cinéma.

On ne croit pas à ce film d'un bout à l'autre: dans la réalité, la violence des élèves et leur impertinence dans nos écoles est beaucoup plus élevée que celle que nous voyons dans ce film.

En regardant ce film on s'ennuie d'un bout à l'autre, il n'arrive rien. Rien. Qu'est-ce qui se passe? Il ne s'est rien passé: pire, dans les classes de nos écoles, de la vie réelle, il se passe autre chose.

Second reviewer

Le film suit une classe de français dans un collège difficile à Paris. Le film est basé sur un excellent livre (*Entre les murs*) de Bégaudeau et filmé super bien par Laurent Cantet.

Les élèves ne sont ni des purs monstres ni tous gentils, ils sont humains, comme le sont les élèves dans nos écoles. Les jeunes acteurs sont formidables dans leurs rôles, si proches de ce qu'ils sont en réalité. Ce film m'a intéressé, et je trouve la fin exceptionnelle.

Quant au prof, interprété par Bégaudeau lui-même, on l'aime bien, il a des idées super démocratiques et idéalistes. Un film difficile à regarder, mais je crois que je n'ai jamais vu un film aussi humain.

First reviewer	Second reviewer
The teacher is bad.	The reviewer likes the teacher: he has democratic and idealistic ideas.
The film and book are bad.	It is based on an excellent book; the film maker has done very well.
It is not believable.	The actors are great, much like students in real life.
In reality, students behave worse than this. In our schools, things are different from this.	The students are neither monsters nor nice; they are human, like students in our schools.
Nothing happens.	The film is interesting or the ending is great.

(any two or three contrasting views)

Chapter 3

How to tackle talking and writing

Talking and writing, the productive skills, are often the ones students are most worried about. However, you should know that over the last few years most students got very good marks for these, as they can be thoroughly prepared for, allowing you to show off what you have learned successfully.

Talking

For this, you need to develop your ability to talk for a minute or so on a topic, have a discussion in French with someone on a couple of topics and make your French sound natural. It might be you and one other person, or you as part of a group. Practising this will allow you to perform better in the final talking assessment. Try recording yourself, either in a sound file or in a short film, so you can look and listen again to how you sound. Examiners prefer you to have a reasonable accent, so try listening to a recording you have, then reading it out yourself. Record this and compare the two versions to help you improve your pronunciation. It works!

Writing

You will have two writing tasks to do for your final grade, so it is worth working on your skills as you go through the course. Both of these pieces of writing will involve you writing 20–30 words in response to each of a number of questions, bullet points or short statements. It really is worth getting into the habit of writing that length of text on a regular basis. That normally would mean two or three short sentences, ideally with a number of conjunctions and clauses in each. You will find more advice on this in Chapter 9 'Writing: The final exam' and Chapter 10 'Writing: The assignment'.

For both of the productive skills of talking and writing you will be assessed on a number of criteria:
- You have said or written something that is relevant.
- You have shown some knowledge and understanding of French in your work (that means variety of language and structures).
- You manage to communicate successfully what you are trying to say (and with some accuracy in writing).
- Your work has a sense of structure.
- Your verbs are pretty accurate.

How do I improve in the four skills?

For reading and listening, it is really a matter of practice. Follow the advice in Chapters 4 and 6, but just give yourself as many opportunities as you can to read and listen to French. Listen to the audio files for this book, then look at the script and listen again, so you get a better feel for what you are listening to.

For talking and writing, we will now give you some ideas for different kinds of activities to help you improve your skills.

Talking

For a presentation or discussion, Chapter 8 will provide you with lots of advice on preparing for the talking assessment; however, getting used to taking part in role play and transactional tasks will help you prepare for the conversation in the talking assessment as well as producing the kind of language you need for the writing task in the final exam.

The role play

This requires polite, formal language (the kind of language you might find in a transaction, a job interview and in a vocational situation). You should use *vous*, *votre*, and the verb forms that go with *vous*, unless the task is specifically a role play between two young people. A transaction will be straightforward to prepare for as the task will be structured. You will know what you are expected to ask and can prepare this thoroughly. In a vocational situation, where the task will be more conversational, you should also follow the guidance given for the conversation assessment in Chapter 8. In this section, we will take you through the preparation for both these types of task. However, remember that most of the advice in the conversation guidelines applies to role play as well, and make sure you have checked out the advice on forming questions in Chapter 8.

The transactional task

We will look at one kind of transactional task but the techniques and much of the advice here can be carried over to other tasks.

Booking a hotel

You are intending to go on holiday to France with your family. You phone a hotel to try to book accommodation. Your teacher or a fellow student will play the part of the person at the hotel. You should know how much you want to pay before you start, and what kind of accommodation you are looking for.

You should carry out the following tasks:
- *Ask if they have rooms available in July.*
- *Ask if they have rooms with a bath/shower.*
- *Give some dates, and ask if the rooms are available then.*
- *Find out if there is a restaurant.*
- *Ask if they have rooms with a balcony.*
- *Ask the cost for: a) rooms b) breakfast.*
- *Ask when breakfast will be served.*
- *Ask where exactly the hotel is.*

Ask if they have rooms available in July.	Remember to start off by introducing yourself and saying why you are calling: *Bonjour, je m'appelle … Je vous téléphone pour …* Be prepared to have to spell your name. You should also know how many rooms you want. *Je cherche deux chambres pour …*
Ask if they have rooms with a bath/shower.	Remember to keep on using *vous*, and to use the correct question form: *Est-ce que vous avez …?* You may be given an option in the answer, such as a price difference, and you should be ready for this.
Give some dates, and ask if the rooms are available then.	This gives you a chance to use a different tense, the conditional. *Nous voudrions arriver le … et rester jusqu'au … Est-ce que vous auriez des chambres pour ces dates?* Again, be ready to accept different dates if offered them, or to ask for an alternative. *Oui, ce serait possible pour nous. / Non, ce ne serait pas possible. Est-ce que nous pourrions arriver le …?*
Find out if there is a restaurant.	Vary the way you ask questions: just use inflection for this one. *Il y a un restaurant à l'hôtel?*
Ask if they have rooms with a balcony.	Try a different form of question, using inversion. *Avez-vous des chambres avec balcon?*
Ask the cost for: a) rooms b) breakfast.	There are lots of ways of asking how much something costs. To vary it, you can just ask if breakfast is included. *Deux chambres avec …, ça coûte combien? Le petit déjeuner est compris dans le prix?* To make your conversation better, repeat the answer and write down the costs. And remember your budget: you might have to ask for cheaper rooms if the prices you are quoted are too high. *Vous avez des chambres moins chères?*
Ask when breakfast will be served.	A straightforward question: *À quelle heure est-ce que le petit déjeuner est servi?* To make your conversation better, repeat the answer and write down the times.
Ask where exactly the hotel is.	Again, a straightforward question, and a chance to note down the answer: *Où se trouve l'hôtel exactement?* And finally, remember to finish off the booking. You could say you will call back to confirm the booking. *Je vous téléphonerai demain pour confirmer.*

The vocational role play

You have an interview for a post as a waiter in France for the summer. Your teacher might play the role of interviewer. You should take the chance to ask some questions, as this will show you are applying knowledge and understanding of French. It will also help you prepare for the task in the final assessment. Some suggestions are added below, but you could make up more if you feel confident.

Comment vous appelez-vous?	Remember to start off by saying Hello! You could also add in your nationality and the answer to the next question. *Bonjour, Monsieur/Madame. Je m'appelle … Je suis écossais(e).*
Comment ça s'écrit?	Know your alphabet!
Quel âge avez-vous?	You could also add in the answer to the next question: *J'ai … ans.*
Votre lieu et date de naissance?	Straightforward, and the chance to add your nationality, if you have not already done so: *Je suis né le … à …*

Vous habitez où?	You can add details about where you live, where exactly it is and your address if you want: *J'habite … en … C'est dans le … Mon adresse, c'est …*
Quel poste voulez-vous?	You know the job, because it is in the instructions. You can add in the bit about your experience here if you want to extend your answer: *Je cherche un poste de serveur/serveuse.*
Vous avez de l'expérience?	A chance to give details if you wish: where you worked, how long for, what you thought of it and so on. *Oui, j'ai déjà travaillé comme … chez …. J'ai travaillé pendant … ans. J'aimais bien mon travail.*
Quelles langues parlez-vous?	Don't just give a list; say how well you speak them and how long you have learned them for: *Je parle couramment/un peu le …. Je l'apprends depuis ….*
Vous avez un petit boulot?	Another chance to give details if you wish: where you work, how long you've been in the job and so on. *Oui, je travaille comme … chez …. J'ai travaillé pendant … ans. J'aime bien mon travail.*
Quelles sont vos qualités personelles?	A chance to say nice things about yourself: *Je suis travailleur/ travailleuse, honnête, et je m'entends bien avec tout le monde.*
Quand est-ce que vous pouvez commencer?	A chance to answer the next question at the same time: *Je pourrais commencer le …. Je veux rester jusqu'au …. Est-ce que cela vous convient?*
Vous voulez rester combien de temps?	See above.
Vous avez des questions?	A chance for you to ask some questions: *Est-ce que je peux loger dans l'hôtel? Combien d'heures est-ce qu'on doit travailler? Il y a beaucoup de travail le week-end? Combien est-ce que je vais gagner?*
	Remember to say goodbye properly: *Alors merci et au revoir, Monsieur/Madame.*

Writing
Planning your writing

If you are writing about something, a description or an opinion piece, then decide what your title will be. Once you have chosen your topic area, focus on the actual language you will use. Try to think of two or three headings to break down the task, so for each part you are writing 25 or so words. Preparing a piece of writing is very much like working on a prepared talk. The dos and don'ts are very similar.

Hints & tips ★

✓ Do look at the textbook or texts you are working from for good ideas you can use.

✓ Do make sure you understand what you are writing — avoid taking chunks of text from a source you don't really understand.

✓ Do use a variety of structures: different tenses, joining words like **parce que** or **quand** to make longer sentences, adjectives, adverbs and phrases you know are correct. ⇨

⇨
✓ Do give your opinion, and prepare different ways of saying what you think. Look at the 'Giving opinions' section in Chapter 11.
✓ Don't always stick to safe, simple language. It may be easier, but won't stretch you to help you get better for the final exam. Try out some of the more impressive sentences you have learned. Note down useful vocabulary and phrases you have seen elsewhere under appropriate topic headings so you can reuse them in your writing.
✓ Don't use lists of things as these will not help you to show structure or knowledge of French. What will be more important than the actual number of words is the number and variety of structures.

To help you develop your writing skills we have selected two possible topics, one using personal language and the other using discursive language. We will guide you through the process involved in preparing for and carrying out the task. The personal language topic could be the basis for a presentation in French on yourself, which you could use to help you prepare for the talk assessment, and the discursive topic could help you prepare for the writing assignment you will carry out as part of the course. You can follow the same pattern for a topic of your own choice, and you might also find Chapter 8 'Talking: Preparing for the assessment' useful when preparing for a specific writing task.

Remember

☞ Make sure you choose work you are familiar with as a source of material.
☞ Make sure you know your writing is correct and the language is accurate.
☞ Include a variety of tenses and structures.
☞ Do the proof reading when you have finished.

Personal language: A letter to a French-speaking friend

You decide to write a letter to a friend in French about how things are in your family. Sort out your ideas and choose the areas you feel most confident about; best of all choose the areas you have been covering in class recently. Think about ways of getting different tenses and structures into your writing. Plan what you are going to write.

Look at the vocabulary in Chapter 12 and take what you think might help you. Also look at the suggested structures in Chapter 11 and take a few you think will fit in with what you are going to say.

Now that you have chosen the kinds of thing you are going to say, let us look at the first section of the letter. After starting with some letter-writing vocabulary, you are going to describe who is in your family. This lets you start with simple language, which you should know is correct.

You can fit in adjectives and verbs with *il* and *elle*. You will be able to use any special phrases you know. You can also introduce a couple of good structures to show you know lots of good French! Here is an example of the kind of thing you can say.

> *Salut Pierre,*
>
> *Ça va? Ici, tout va bien. Tu m'as demandé de te parler un peu de ma famille. Chez nous, il y a mon père Lewis, ma mère Helen et mes deux frères. Mon père a 38 ans, et il a les cheveux bruns et courts. Helen, ma mère, est petite et mince. Mon père travaillait comme facteur, mais maintenant il a un poste dans un bureau. Ma mère n'a jamais travaillé, car elle a trois enfants!*

This would be a straightforward start and makes it easy to be accurate. The second section could go on to talk about how you get on with your parents. This paragraph can include a past tense. It allows you to give opinions and to demonstrate your knowledge and understanding of French. Here is an example of what you could write.

> *Je m'entends bien avec mon père, parce que nous aimons tous les deux le football, et aussi parce qu'il me donne mon argent de poche! J'ai toujours aimé ma mère, car elle m'aidait beaucoup quand j'avais des problèmes à l'école.*

This adds to your writing and shows a variety of tenses and structures. Finally, you could prepare a section on a problem you have to allow you to get even more variety in. This is the kind of thing you might write.

> *Mon seul problème est que je n'ai pas assez de liberté. Mes parents n'aiment pas quand je sors le soir et le week-end. Ils préfèrent que je reste à la maison! Quelle barbe! Alors, je vais parler de mon école la prochaine fois. Et toi, comment est ta famille?*
>
> *Au revoir,*

These three paragraphs make up about 170 words, which is a good number of words to be writing at National 5 level.

Discursive writing: *La télévision*

This will allow you to write about a topic and use lots of opinion words as well as good phrases from the texts you are working from. Your first task should be to look at your source texts and select some bits. Then break your task into sections. You could use a section in which you talk about what you watch, then have a section in which you talk about what other young people in your class do (allowing you to put in third person verbs). You could finish off by writing about the dangers of too much television and not enough exercise.

The first section might read something like this.

> *Je ne regarde pas beaucoup de télé, car je n'ai pas le temps avec le sport et mes devoirs. Je regarde un feuilleton tous les soirs avant de dîner, et le week-end je regarde quelquefois du foot ou un film. Mon programme favori, c'est une ancienne série américaine qui s'appelle 'Buffy contre les*

vampires'. J'ai toujours regardé Buffy, car j'adore Sarah Michelle Gellar, l'actrice qui joue Buffy!

This gives you a total of almost 70 words, and has a past tense in it as well as an opinion and a reason.

> *Mes copains aussi regardent peu la télé, mais bien sûr nous avons tous passé des heures devant la télé quand nous étions plus jeunes. On regardait tous les feuilletons et on en discutait le lendemain à l'école.*

You have the chance to demonstrate a variety of tenses and verb structures here, and show that you have a good knowledge of more than the basics. In the final section you have the chance to show ways of expressing opinions and giving reasons for them.

> *Il faut penser aux dangers pour les jeunes de regarder trop la télé. Nous savons déjà que nos jeunes mangent trop de fast-food. Je trouve dangereux de combiner le fast-food avec un manque d'exercice. Nous devons encourager les jeunes à penser à leur santé, sinon nous aurons de grands problèmes dans le futur!*

Basic grammar

When marking your work, teachers will be looking for accuracy in basic structures. That means straightforward, simple language, and you should be able to show you can do everything listed below at least.

What you should know

Verbs

★ Use the correct form of the verb. This includes using subject pronouns (like *je, il, elle*) and correct verb endings, matching the subject.
★ Use *ne … pas, ne … jamais*, etc.
★ Ask simple questions correctly.
★ Use 'modal' verbs, such as *vouloir* and *pouvoir*, and the auxiliary verbs *avoir* and *être*.
★ Use verbs fairly accurately in personal language and polite language. This includes the correct polite verb forms for requests (*voulez-vous …, je voudrais …*) and also the correct verb forms for plural subjects: *mes sœurs ont …, mes amis sont …*
★ Use present, future, imperfect, perfect and conditional tenses.

Nouns

★ Use the correct type of article/determiner (*un/une/des, le/la/les, ce/cette/ces*) and, if you can, the correct form (for example, correct gender or number).

$\Rightarrow$

* ★ Use nouns with the correct gender form of article and adjective.
* ★ Use the words for 'my' and 'your' correctly.

Pronouns

* ★ Use the correct form of subject or object pronouns, and put them in the correct place.

Prepositions

* ★ Use the correct preposition, and know what it does to articles and pronouns (*à* and *le = au, pour* and *je = pour moi*).

How do I go about learning vocabulary?

The best way to revise is to practise. Although different people have different ways of learning vocabulary, the following ways might be useful to you.

Hints & tips

* ✓ Try writing out a list of words, then reading them out. Cover up the French words, and see if you can remember the words in English, and of course the other way round.
* ✓ Read things over several times on different occasions.
* ✓ Check your memorising by either covering one part and remembering the other, or by getting someone to do it with you (friend or parent). If you have someone to help you, get them to say a word in English, which you have to put into French.
* ✓ Try to get your words organised into areas, so they all hang together and make sense to you.
* ✓ Use spidergrams of related words.

Chapter 4

Reading at National 5

Introduction

Reading is worth 30 marks, or 25 per cent of your overall mark. It will be tested in the external exam. The reading paper will be handed out to you at the same time as the writing paper and you will have 1 hour 30 minutes for both in total. Give yourself about an hour for the reading paper and 30 minutes for the writing paper. You can choose which order you would like to do them in, but consider starting off with the writing. There will be three texts in the reading paper, each up to 200 words long. That means about 20 minutes for each one. The questions will be in English. Some will be straightforward questions asking for details from the text. You will sometimes be asked to fill in gaps in a sentence or answer a multiple choice question. Make sure you tick the right number of boxes!

You will be able to use a dictionary for this exam, so you need to be very confident about how to use one. Make sure you look at the guide to using a dictionary on pages 26–27 before you start answering questions, especially if you ever find a dictionary annoying!

The key to this assessment is finding the correct answer, and ignoring the bits you do not need. Reading is a skill, and a skill you need to work on to allow you to give your best in the final exam. The way to succeed is to extract from the text what you actually need for your answers and ignore the rest. The exam will test your ability to extract relevant information from the text. That means there is a lot of material that is irrelevant and which you do not need. The skill you have to develop is the skill of identifying which bits you actually need.

There is a sequence you should follow:
1 Read the information in English about the text at the start. This should give you clues as to what the answers are going to be about. Keep this information in your head as you answer the questions.
2 Now look at the questions. These should tell you where in the passage to look for your answers. Look for clue words in the question that will show you where the answer is to be found.
3 Only now should you look at the text. Skim through it to get an idea of what it is about, without using a dictionary.
4 Now look for the key areas that match your questions, and start looking for the answers there. Remember the questions will follow the same order as the text, so you should not have to jump around all over the place.

Let us look at a couple of actual SQA questions and see how this would work in practice.

Example 1

You read the following article about a type of school in Marseille, un lycée professionnel.

Trouver son premier emploi n'est jamais simple. Il est parfois difficile de persuader un employeur d'embaucher des jeunes, surtout si leur expérience professionnelle est limitée ou s'ils n'ont pas assez de qualifications.

Un lycée professionnel à Marseille essaie de résoudre ce problème. Le directeur explique: « Nous offrons un programme où les élèves travaillent chaque matin dans une entreprise et l'après-midi ils ont des cours au lycée. »

Elena est élève dans ce lycée et elle donne son avis sur ce programme: « Moi, je fréquente cette école depuis quinze mois. À mon avis c'est une très bonne façon d'apprendre. Les profs nous traitent comme des adultes, on acquière plus de confiance en soi et en plus on gagne un peu d'argent pour payer les sorties. Le seul inconvénient est que je dois utiliser les transports en commun car l'entreprise se trouve loin de chez moi. »

Ce genre de programme est aussi très avantageux pour les employeurs car ils savent que l'élève a déjà suivi une bonne formation et qu'il sait travailler en équipe.

Questions

1 Why is it sometimes difficult to persuade an employer to employ young people? **2**
    ....
    ....

2 What programme does the *lycée professionnel* offer to its students? Complete the sentence. **2**
    In the morning the students .... and in the afternoon
    they ....

3 **a)** How long has Elena been at the school? **1**
    ....

    b) Why does she think it is a good way to learn? State any **two** things. **2**
    ....
    ....

    c) What is the only disadvantage she says there is? **1**
    ....

4 What are the advantages of this type of programme for employers? State **two** things. **2**
    ....

Reading **question 1**, you should note the key words 'difficult' and 'employer'. Go to the passage and find the words: the answers will be after that. There are two marks available so you have to find two things. In fact, the two things are two phrases, separated by *ou* (or): *si leur expérience professionnelle est limitée* and *s'ils n'ont pas assez de qualifications*. Now write them down in English:

- if they have limited (or not much) (professional) experience
- if they don't have enough qualifications.

In **question 2** you see the word 'programme'. You also have the guidelines for the answer, so you know exactly where to look. Again, there are two marks so there must be two things: *travaillent (chaque matin) dans une entreprise* and *ils ont des cours au lycée*. You should be careful with the first part of the answers because *entreprise* is a false friend. It does not mean 'enterprise', but 'business'. And if you have to look up *cours* make sure you get the right meaning – 'lessons'.

Question 3 (a) is worth only one mark and asks about time: how long. You should look for Elena's name and then follow the text until you see a time: *quinze mois*. Make sure you get the number right!

Question 3 (b) asks for two things and you can easily find the sentence with the answers, but note that three reasons are given in the text! Choose the two reasons you are most certain of and don't try to give all three in your answer. *Les profs nous traitent comme des adultes, on acquière plus de confiance en soi et en plus on gagne un peu d'argent pour payer les sorties.*

- The teachers treat them as adults.
- They get more self-confidence.
- They earn some money (to pay for going out).

Question 3 (c) is worth only one mark and you are asked for a disadvantage: *inconvénient*. Don't write out the whole sentence for one mark: *je dois utiliser les transports en commun* (I have to use public transport) is enough. If you look up *transport* or *commun* in the dictionary and read down the entry a bit you will find the phrase *transports en commun*.

Question 4 asks for two things. Note there is no 'any', so there are only two. Make sure you give enough detail.

- They have had good training.
- They know how to work in a team.

Example 2

In a magazine you read an article about the town of Dreux.

À minuit, au lit!

À minuit, on doit rentrer se coucher! C'est ce qu'a décidé Gérard Hamel, le maire de Dreux, pour les enfants de moins de douze ans.

Pendant tout l'été, les moins de douze ans n'ont pas le droit d'être dans la rue, entre minuit et six heures du matin, s'ils ne sont pas accompagnés d'un adulte. C'est pour protéger les jeunes enfants de tous les dangers de la rue, la nuit, explique le maire. Mais il ne veut pas arrêter là. À l'automne, il voudrait priver les parents de leurs *aides sociales s'ils ne surveillent pas leurs enfants.

Gérard Hamel sait qu'il est soutenu par une bonne partie de la population. Vendredi après-midi, dans la Grande Rue, les avis concordaient. « C'est une bonne chose. En tant que mère de famille, je trouve anormal que les jeunes enfants soient seuls dans les rues toute la nuit », affirme Betty, 25 ans, mère d'un petit garçon.

Dreux est une ville qui est très touchée par le chômage. On connaît des problèmes comme les vols et les agressions. Mais interdire aux plus jeunes d'être dans la rue après minuit, est-ce que cela serait une solution? Le plan, qui a de fortes chances d'être jugé illégal, choque les syndicats de police. « Nous n'ignorons ni les règlements, ni les textes concernant la protection des mineurs, ni la conduite à tenir », souligne le Syndicat National des Policiers.

*aides sociales – *social security payments*

Questions ?

1 The mayor of Dreux has decided to introduce a curfew for children. Give any **three** details of the scheme. **3**

....

....

....

2 Why has he decided to take this action? **1**

....

⇨

3 How does he intend to penalise parents who do not supervise their children? **1**

....

4 What does Betty think of the plan? **2**

....

....

5 State any **two** social problems which exist in Dreux. **2**

....

....

6 What do the police unions think might happen to the plan? **1**

....

....

For **question 1**, by looking at the first paragraph, words like *décidé*, *maire* and *enfants* show you that this is an introduction. So you should look for answers after this. The sentence *Pendant tout l'été, les moins de douze ans n'ont pas le droit d'être dans la rue, entre minuit et six heures du matin, s'ils ne sont pas accompagnés d'un adulte* is where you should start looking. You should see if you can find three details. The first thing to look for is the verbs: *n'ont pas* and *ne sont pas accompagnés* are the two in this sentence. They 'have not' and they 'are not accompanied'. Your next question is who: *les moins de douze ans* tells you the answer is twelve year olds. You might look up *moins*, which is 'less'. Remembering the context, you should work out that this phrase means 'children less than twelve years old'. You should also be able to identify *adulte*, to work out 'not accompanied by an adult'. The next question is what: 'They have not' what? *le droit*. Look it up in the dictionary and you will find 'law' and also 'right'. Immediately after this comes 'to be in the street'. This should enable you to work out the second of the marks. You should also be able to work out times, for a third mark, and the season, for a fourth mark. So, for three marks, any three of these:

- during the summer
- under twelves don't have the right to be in the street
- between midnight and 6a.m.
- when not accompanied by an adult.

Question 2 follows on. The phrase *explique le maire* (the mayor explains) shows you that this is the answer. Again, look for the verb first: *protéger*. If you don't know it, look it up in your dictionary: 'protect'. Looking at the rest of the sentence, it should be clear that the answer is:

- to protect children from the dangers of the street.

To answer **question 3**, look for 'parents' and 'supervise'. When you find them, you will also find a phrase which is translated in the glossary. You now need to look for the verb, which is *priver*. If you don't know it, look it up: 'deprive'. Jumble together all the words that you know, and you should come up with: 'deprive the parents of their social security payments', which you can turn into the more English-sounding:

- take away from the parents their social security payments.

For **question 4**, look for Betty's name, then inside the quotation marks you will find her ideas. *C'est une bonne chose* is her first opinion, then after *je trouve* you can find the second opinion. You might look up *anormal* if you can't guess it means 'abnormal', but in *que les jeunes enfants soient seuls dans les rues toute la nuit* you should find all the key words – 'young children', 'alone', 'streets', 'all night' – to give you your answer.

Question 5 asks you for social problems, i.e. things, so for this question you don't look for verbs, but for nouns. In the next paragraph you can find *le chômage, les vols et les aggressions*. If you don't know the words, look them up to get two words (that is all you need):

- unemployment
- thefts
- attacks/violence.

Remember

☞ Only look up what you have to.
☞ Know where to look for the answer.
☞ Know what you are looking for – verbs and nouns are the two most important things.

For **question 6**, look for the words *police* and *plan* to help you see where to find the answer. You can find the phrase *a de fortes chances d'être déclaré illégal* so you should be able to work out it means it may be declared illegal. Use bits from the text as your evidence but write them *in English*!

The other major skill needed for reading exams is using a dictionary. It is very easy to spend far too long looking up words, and also very easy to find the wrong answer. What is worse, sometimes you cannot find any answer. It is usual to blame the dictionary for this, but more often than not it is the person looking up the word who has got it wrong. Make sure you know your alphabet properly, and practise using the dictionary.

Remember

Using a dictionary

☞ When you find a word, it is followed in many dictionaries by the guide to pronouncing it. There might also be a word that tells you what different contexts the translation is valid for, or 'prep', which is telling you it is a preposition.
☞ There will often be several entries for a word, because some words are both verb and noun, with different meanings.

☞ Because French verbs have endings, you will often not find exactly the word you are looking for; you need the infinitive.

☞ Don't just look at the start of the entry, go on down the entry to see if something further down makes sense.

☞ Always keep in mind the context of the passage you are reading as it may well help you find the correct phrase in a dictionary.

☞ Watch for the little bracketed words in some dictionaries like '(sport)', which tell you what context the word is used in.

☞ Sometimes it makes sense to look up words in the English half of the dictionary to give you a clue as to where to look for the answer to a question.

If the question asks for two things, just give two things. The examiner can only give you marks for two things. You are wasting time if you write more than is necessary in an answer.

What you should know

Vocabulary

There are some vocabulary areas that always come up in the exam. It is important that you know and are able to recognise these words as it will save time if you do not need to look them up in the dictionary in the exam:

★ numbers, including times, dates, temperatures, distances and prices
★ days, months, weeks and years
★ question words and phrases.

The three texts in the exam will come from three of the contexts of **society**, **learning**, **employability** and **culture**. The fourth context will be covered in your listening assessment. Below are some texts you can try to work on from each of the four contexts.

Society: Lifestyles 1

You read this article about the health of French people.

Imaginez une pilule miracle … une pilule énergisante, qui aiderait à contrôler des problèmes de santé comme les maladies cardiaques, le diabète, l'obésité, certains types de cancer, la dépression, l'arthrite, etc.

Question

1 What could this miracle pill do? **1**

....

Eh bien, bonne nouvelle: cette pilule miracle existe. Son nom: l'exercice! De source naturelle (ne contient aucun agent chimique ni additif), elle doit être consommée une fois par jour à l'heure de votre choix et il est préférable de la savourer pendant au moins trente minutes pour retirer le maximum de profits; elle se présente sous différentes formes (marche, patinage, natation, ski, jogging, bicyclette); elle peut se prendre autant à l'intérieur qu'à l'extérieur; et elle peut même parfois remplacer d'autres pilules.

Questions ?

2 How often and when should the miracle medicine be taken? **2**

....
....

3 What special advantages does the pill have? **2**

....

Les faits sont là. Pourtant, nous sommes confrontés à une évidence: l'activité physique régulière apporte des effets bénéfiques sur la santé mais plus de la moitié des Français sont inactifs ou ne sont pas suffisamment actifs pour en retirer ces bienfaits.

Question

4 Why is there a problem for French people? State **two** things. **2**

....
....

En plus, il faut limiter la consommation de sel, qui favorise l'apparition de la cellulite.

Comme minimum, on doit faire trente minutes d'activités physiques, au moins trois fois par semaine. Et pour la santé, on ne doit jamais manger debout.

Question

5   The article gives guidelines in the final three pieces of advice. Complete the blanks. **3**
    You should limit

    ....

    It encourages you to

    ....

    For your health, you should

    ....

Society: Lifestyles 2

Bien manger est essentiel à notre bien-être

Malheureusement, nous manquons parfois de temps durant la pause déjeuner. Au lieu d'aller à la cantine à midi, et de faire la queue, plus sympa d'aller au fast-food du coin entre copains.

On a besoin de quatre repas par jour: un petit déjeuner complet, un déjeuner, un goûter/collation à 16h et un dîner. Manger toutes les quatre heures, surtout pas entre ces repas. Mais la plupart des adolescents n'ont pas faim le matin, et mangent mal à midi.

Questions ?

1   What effect does a lack of time at midday have on people's habits? State **two** things. **2**

    ....

    ....

2   What does the article say the **two** problems are for young people's healthy eating? **2**

    ....

    ....

La solution?

Pour être en bonne forme, mange un peu de tout aux bonnes heures. Si au petit matin le temps manque, prends des aliments à base de céréales. Des paquets individuels que l'on peut emporter partout, que tu peux manger à la récréation de 10 heures. Ils apportent des éléments nutritifs dont l'organisme a besoin pour bien « fonctionner ». Un fruit pour les vitamines sera parfait (meilleur qu'un jus de fruit classique, il y a plus de sucre), ou du lait pour le calcium. Les deux, c'est encore mieux.

Questions ?

3 The article gives advice to people who have no time for breakfast. Are the following statements **true** or **false**? Write T or F in the boxes below. **3**

Take a cereal bar with you.	
Their effect lasts up to 10 hours.	
They provide nutrition that your body needs.	

4 What should you add to this? State **two** things. **2**

....

....

À midi, si vraiment le temps presse, un sandwich peut être envisagé. Une soupe de légumes avec, ou un fruit comme dessert. Si on choisit le fast-food, mangez léger le soir.

Question ?

5 If you choose to eat fast food, what should you then do? **1**

....

Learning: In context

This article is written to give advice on how to improve your language learning.

Comment mieux apprendre une langue?

Pas de doute, la façon la plus efficace d'apprendre une langue étrangère, c'est d'aller dans le pays en question. Une recette que John, Américain installé en France, applique à la lettre: « je lis le journal en français tous les jours, je parle avec beaucoup de gens, je regarde des films, des émissions, des pubs … tout en français ». Certes une immersion totale pendant quelques semaines marche, si on peut le payer.

Question ?

1 How does John apply the advice given? State **three** things. **3**

....

....

....

Mais il est possible d'améliorer son niveau de langue depuis son canapé, devant sa télé ou son ordinateur! Comment faire? Regarder la télé en anglais et aller voir des films en version originale, c'est rapidement efficace. Trouver un correspondant à l'étranger! Il faut ensuite échanger régulièrement par mail ou par téléphone avec lui ou elle, et puis pourquoi pas essayer d'organiser des séjours linguistiques avec ce correspondant?

Questions ?

2   What is the first suggestion for people who stay at home? State **two** things. **2**

....

....

3   If you find a pen pal, what **two** suggestions does the article make? **2**

....

....

L'autre bonne méthode: certains centres proposent des cours de conversation. Le principe de ces séances? Elles ont lieu en présence d'un ou d'une native du pays de la langue en question. En plus de la discussion, ces rencontres donnent l'occasion d'approfondir la culture du pays en question. Pour les trouver, il faut se renseigner près de chez soi et en ligne, sur les blogs des expatriés par exemple.

Questions ?

4   How do the conversation classes work? State **two** things. **2**

....

....

5   What is the difference between the first and the later pieces of advice? **1**

....

Employability: Jobs

This article tells us how French universities (in this case Écoles) are trying to make their students international.

Les stages à l'étranger

Intégrer l'internationalisation des entreprises dans leur cursus, c'est l'objectif des *Business Schools* françaises, les Écoles de Management. Dans 80% des écoles, les étudiants doivent effectuer un séjour hors de France.

⇨

Pas une école qui ne propose à ses étudiants d'aller étudier dans une université à l'étranger, pour une durée entre trois mois et deux semestres. Cela constitue une expérience indispensable pour accéder à la connaissance d'autres cultures, d'autres modes de pensée en plus des acquis linguistiques essentiels. Parfois, ce stage intervient dès la première année, comme à l'École de Management de Lyon. C'est l'occasion de réaliser un projet personnel avant de se spécialiser.

Questions ?

1 What must students do in 80% of business schools? **1**

....

2 How long is this normally for? **2**

....

3 State **two** benefits it brings. **2**

....

....

4 What is different in Lyon? **1**

....

Les destinations à favoriser

Ceux qui parlent anglais ont tout intérêt à se diriger vers un pays anglophone. Les États-Unis et le Canada restent les destinations les plus demandées. De même que les pays nordiques, où les cours sont assurés en anglais.

« On incite actuellement nos étudiants à se diriger vers la Chine ou l'Inde », affirme Jean-Louis Scaringella, directeur général de l'ESCP-EAP.

Question ?

5 Why might French students choose to go to a Scandinavian university? **1**

....

L'Essec propose même une formule alliant apprentissage et expatriation: une partie du stage se déroule en France, le reste dans une filiale de l'entreprise à l'étranger.

Grenoble École de Management organise, elle, un projet « tour du monde »: chaque année, quinze étudiants partent neuf mois sur cinq continents et financent leur projet en réalisant des études de marché pour le compte d'universités et d'entreprises.

Questions

6 The ESSEC model is different. Complete the sentences below. **2**
   Part of the course ....
   The rest in a branch ....
7 How long do the students spend abroad? **1**
   ....

Culture: Planning a trip

Petits trucs pour voyageurs en solo

Étudiez votre destination

Le mieux, pour commencer, est de prendre des renseignements sur le pays. Pour le premier voyage, on vous conseille de commencer par un pays « facile », c'est-à-dire où il y a des moyens de communication faciles à utiliser et des infrastructures. Exemple: Amérique du Nord, Europe, Asie du Sud-Est.

Questions

1 The author recommends an 'easy' country for a first trip. What might that mean? **1**
   ....
2 Apart from Europe, where else does he recommend? **1**
   ....

Mettez vos papiers en lieu sûr

Vos papiers et votre argent sont ce que vous aurez de plus précieux (mis à part votre sourire). Prenez-en soin. Avant le départ, scannez vos papiers et billets d'avion et copiez-les sur votre boîte mail ou une clé USB. Pendant votre voyage, ne les quittez jamais. Vous pouvez acheter une pochette pour les objets de valeur que vous mettrez sous votre T-shirt; ainsi en cas de vol ou de pluie torrentielle, vos papiers seront toujours là. La nuit, gardez-les près de vous, au pied du sac du couchage, peut-être.

Questions ?

3 What should you do before you set off? State **two** things. **2**

....

....

4 The writer gives advice about a pouch or purse. Are the following statements **true** or **false**? Write T or F in the boxes below. **3**

You could wear it under your t-shirt.	
Your papers are with you if you are flying in heavy rain.	
Give it to a guard at night.	

Voyagez léger

Votre sac va vous suivre partout. Préparez-le bien. Un vêtement de pluie, de bonnes chaussures, les papiers, un bon petit dictionnaire, une carte de la région. On conseille aussi un couteau … ça peut toujours servir dans n'importe quelle situation. N'oubliez pas non plus la crème solaire, les lunettes de soleil … et les produits anti-moustiques. Le plus important dans tous les cas, et où que vous alliez: pas trop. Avoir un sac qui n'est pas trop lourd, c'est essentiel, cela fera une différence.

Questions ?

5 The writer gives a list of things you should not forget. State any **one** of them. **1**

....

....

6 What is the most important advice about luggage? **2**

....

....

Culture: Other countries

You read this article about a woman who got on in the world.

Adrienne Clarkson, gouverneure générale du Canada

J'ai débarqué au Canada avec ma famille en 1942. J'avais trois ans. Avec d'autres réfugiés de Hong Kong, nous avions voyagé à bord d'un bateau de la Croix-Rouge. Je me souviens encore des bombes japonaises qui pleuvaient sur la ville. Nous avions peu d'argent, et notre nouvelle vie à Ottawa n'a jamais été facile. Mon père me répétait qu'il fallait travailler pour obtenir quelque chose sur cette terre. Dès que j'ai été en âge de travailler, mes parents m'ont encouragée à prendre un petit emploi.

Question ?

1 Why was her early life difficult? State **three** things. **3**

....
....
....

À 17 ans, mon secondaire terminé, j'ai décroché un emploi dans un bureau. Comme personne ne savait exactement en quoi consistait ma fonction, j'ai décidé d'en faire le plus possible. Je répondais au téléphone, j'écoutais les réclamations des clients et j'apprenais à être toujours accueillante. Personne ne m'avait imposé ces besognes. Je savais seulement que, si j'assumais de plus en plus de responsabilités, je finirais par me rendre indispensable à mes employeurs.

Questions ?

2 What tasks did she decide to take on in her work? State **two** things. **2**

....
....

3 Why did she decide to take these on? Give details. **2**

....
....

Huit ans plus tard, quand j'ai commencé à travailler à la télévision, je n'ai jamais refusé une tâche, si humble soit-elle. De tous les gens avec qui j'ai collaboré à la télévision, ceux dont je garde le meilleur souvenir sont ceux qui étaient capables de mettre l'épaule à la roue quand c'était nécessaire. Aujourd'hui, lorsque je vois quelqu'un prendre des initiatives, je souris en me disant: « En voilà un qui connaît le secret du travail: si tu veux faire ton chemin en ce monde, rends-toi indispensable. »

Questions ?

4 Who does she remember best from her days in television? Give details. **2**

....

....

5 Overall, what does she think is the secret of getting on at work? **1**

....

....

Society: Lifestyles 1

1 help control health problems
2 once a day, for at least 30 minutes, whenever you choose
  (any two)
3 has no additives; comes in lots of forms; can be taken indoors or out; can replace other pills
  (any two)
4 more than half of French people are inactive; or not active enough to get the benefits
5 limit salt intake; do 30 minutes exercise at least three times a week; never eat standing up

Society: Lifestyles 2
Bien manger est essentiel à notre bien-être

1 people don't want to queue; they go to a fast-food place with pals
2 they aren't hungry in the morning; they eat badly at lunchtime
3

Take a cereal bar with you.	T
Their effect lasts up to 10 hours.	F
They provide nutrition that your body needs.	T

4 a piece of fruit; a drink of milk
5 eat something light in the evening

Learning: In context
Comment mieux apprendre une langue?

1 he reads a French newspaper daily; he speaks to lots of people; he watches films/television/ adverts in French
2 to watch television in English/to see films without dubbing (in the original language)
3 write (or email) or phone regularly; try to organise an exchange visit

4 there is a native speaker; people discuss things
5 the first one you will have to pay for, the other two are less expensive or the first one involves going abroad, the other two don't

Employability: Jobs
Les stages à l'étranger

1 students must spend some time out of France/abroad
2 between 3 months and two terms
3 you learn about other cultures; you learn about other ways of thinking; you gain language skills
  (any two)
4 students go in their first year at university
5 their courses are held in English
6 part of the course takes place in a company in France; the rest in a branch abroad
7 nine months

Culture: Planning a trip
Petits trucs pour voyageurs en solo

1 an 'easy' country has means of communication that are easy to use/a good infrastructure
  (either one)
2 North America and South East Asia
  (both)
3 scan your papers and plane tickets; put them in your mailbox or on a memory stick
4

You could wear it under your t-shirt.	T
Your papers are with you even if you are flying in heavy rain.	F
Give it to a guard at night.	F

5 suncream, sunglasses, anti-mosquito products
  (any one)
6 don't take too much; your bag shouldn't be too heavy

Culture: Other countries
Adrienne Clarkson, gouverneure générale du Canada

1 she was a refugee; she was bombed by the Japanese; they had little money

2 she answered the phone; listened to customer complaints; worked at being welcoming (any two)

3 if she took on responsibilities, her employers would find she was indispensable

4 people who could work hard (put their shoulder to the wheel) when it was needed

5 if you want to get on, make yourself indispensable/people who take the initiative succeed

Listening at National 5

Introduction

Listening is worth 20 marks, or 25 per cent of your overall result. It will be tested in the external exam, and the test will last up to 30 minutes. You will not be able to use a dictionary for this exam, so you need to be prepared for the exam in advance and make sure you know the basic vocabulary that comes up again and again.

The paper will be in two parts. The first part will be a monologue, or just one person talking about a subject. You will hear this three times and be asked to answer some questions on what has been said. There are eight marks for this. There will then follow a discussion or dialogue between two people talking about the same topic area. You will also hear this three times. You will then have to answer questions about what has been said. There are twelve marks for this. The answers to the questions will be found in the part spoken by the person who is doing most of the talking, so remember to listen particularly well when she or he is speaking.

To help with your revision, the listening questions in this guide are broken into contexts. In the real exam, you will not know in advance which context will turn up. The dialogues and solo talks here are separate, so you can listen to them at different times.

Try not to write anything down during the first listening, even if you know the answer; you will have plenty of time later. It is very tempting to dash things down so that you do not forget them, but realistically that is not going to happen. You also risk missing out important details because you are concentrating on writing. Use that first listening to make sure you hear everything, and to give you an idea of which bits you have to listen to extra carefully the next time in order to pick up the details you are required to give in your answer.

Make sure you know what you are listening for. There will be lots of information you do not need, which just acts as interference when you are listening. Focus on what is needed for the answer. That means reading the questions before you hear the recording. You only have to keep your concentration solid for the few minutes the recording is playing, so make sure you do.

If you are not sure of an answer, go ahead and guess, as what you guess will be a secret between the examiner and you. Try, however, to make it an intelligent guess. If what you have written looks daft to you, then it probably is; your answer should make sense.

If the answer asks for two things, just give two things. The examiner can only give you marks for two things. Writing more than necessary takes up valuable time. Try to have your answers clear by the end of the second listening, and use the third listening to check them.

Hints & tips

Here are some other steps to take that should help you do your best:

✓ When you are told to open your paper, do so and read the information at the start setting the scene.

✓ Draw a line to the left of the centre of the page and put your notes on the left of the page when it is time. You should transfer your final answers to the right of the line at the end, and score out your notes with a single line.

✓ Read all the questions carefully, as this will prepare you for what the dialogue is about.

What you should know

Vocabulary

There are some vocabulary areas that always trip people up in the listening exam:

★ numbers, including times, dates, temperatures, distances and prices
★ days, months, weeks and years
★ school, including subjects.

It is important that you feel confident in these key areas so that you do not miss out on easy marks.

Visit www.hoddergibson.co.uk and click on 'Updates & extras' to download the audio files for the listening tasks in this book.

Monologues

Society: Media

🔊 *You will hear a young French actor who started working while still at school. Listen to what she says and then answer the questions.*

Questions

1   Louise is a teenage film star. How old was she when she started? **1**

   ....

2   Why has her television role finished? **1**

   ....

3   She is going to make a film next. Complete the sentences. **2**
   It is about a family who ....
   The film will take place in ....

4   Where will she stay while she is there? Give **three** details. **3**

   ....
   ....
   ....

5   Where might she like to go to university afterwards? **1**

   ....

Learning

🔊 *You will hear a French schoolboy talking to you about his experiences at school. Listen to what he says and then answer the questions.*

Questions ❓

1 What does he do in the middle of the day? **1**

....

2 He tells you about his homework. Complete the sentences. **2**
I do homework for ....
I have no one to help me, so ....

3 What reasons does he give for liking school? Give **two** details. **2**

....

....

4 How does he describe his English teacher? **1**

....

5 He gives two comparisons with schools in Scotland. What does he say about the two systems? **2**
His day ....
The holidays ....

Employability

🔊 *You will hear a French student talking about his plans for the future. Listen to what he says and then answer the questions.*

Questions ❓

1 Philippe says he did not like school much. Give **two** reasons. **2**

....

....

2 He has chosen to go to university in Nice. Complete the sentences. **2**
The University of Nice ....
Moreover, the town of Nice ....

3 Where is he going to stay in Nice? State **two** details. **2**

....

....

4 Overall, he knows he will work to support himself at university. Complete the sentences. **2**
This summer he will ....
In Nice he will look for a job to ....

Culture

🔊 *You will hear a young French student talking about her visit to South America. Listen to what she says and then answer the questions.*

Questions ❓

1 Lucie went to South America. Why did she go there? State **two** things. **2**

....

....

2 Where exactly did she go? **1**

....

3 While she was there she stayed in different kinds of accommodation. Complete the sentences. **2**
She spent the first month...
When she was in the real south, mostly she..

4 She mentions some problems she had there. Are the following statements **true** or **false**? Write T or F in the boxes below. **2**

She did not mind the cold temperature.	
Once all her things got soaked by the rain.	

5 Complete the sentence. **1**
Most of all, she liked the journey because ....

Dialogues

Society

🔊 *Amélie and Christophe are discussing* Nouvelle Star, *a television talent show in France. Listen to what they say and then answer the questions.*

Questions ❓

1 What does Amélie have to say about the return of *Nouvelle Star*? Complete the sentences. **3**
For her it was ....
It has not been on ....
It is ....

2 Christophe does not like it; he thinks it is all fake. How does Amélie respond? Give details. **2**

....

....

3 Christophe says most participants have no chance of succeeding. Amélie replies to this. Are the following statements **true** or **false**? Write T or F in the boxes below. **3**

It is horrible the way they show people who cannot sing.	
People laugh at them.	
The singers find it amusing seeing themselves on television.	

4 Amélie mentions Christophe Willem. Complete the sentences. **2**
Christophe Willem, for example,...
Every show he..

5 What different things will Amélie and Christophe do this weekend? **2**

....

....

Learning

🔊 *Richard, who is French but is attending a Scottish school, and his cousin Adrienne are discussing the schools they go to. Listen to what they say and then answer the questions.*

Questions ?

1 Adrienne asks Richard how he finds his new school. State **three** differences he finds. **3**

....

....

....

2 Adrienne finds the school rugby team surprising. What does Richard answer? Complete the sentences. **3**

It is ....

The school has ....

It is organised by...

3 Adrienne does not think much of this. How does Richard answer? Give details. **2**

....

....

4 What differences does Richard find with homework? State **two** things. **2**

....

....

5 Richard finds **two** disadvantages in his new school. What are they? **2**

....

....

Employability

🔊 *Marc and Hélène are discussing the work experience (stage en entreprise) she has recently completed. During work experience in France, the employer provides a link person (un tuteur) who helps students when they are at work. Listen to what they say and then answer the questions.*

Questions ?

1 Why did Hélène like her work experience? State **three** things. **3**

....

....

....

2 How did she start off her placement? Complete the sentences. **3**

She made contact with ....

After that she ....

Her tutor ....

3 What did Hélène ask about before she started work? State any **two** things. **2**

....

....

⇨

⇨

4 How did she finish off her placement? **1**

....

5 Hélène is keeping in contact with her tutor. Are the following statements **true** or **false**? Write T or F in the boxes below. **3**

She discussed her placement with her tutor and her boss.	
She has written a thank you letter to her tutor.	
He will help her with her exams.	

Culture

🔊 *Caroline and Daniel are discussing Caroline's summer holidays. Listen to what they have to say and then answer the questions.*

Questions ❓

1 What are Caroline's plans for the summer? State **three** things. **3**

....

....

....

2 Why is she doing this? Complete the sentences. **3**

She has started ....

She always likes to be ....

She would like to travel ....

3 Daniel asks why she does not go to England. Caroline replies. Which three of the following statements are **true?** Write T in the boxes below. **3**

She wanted to visit Scotland.	
She was there two years ago.	
She does not like English.	
Italy is more important for her right now.	
The weather will be better there.	

4 Daniel's response is she wants a suntan. What is she actually looking forward to on her holiday? State **three** things. **3**

....

....

....

Monologues

Society: Media

Tout a commencé quand j'avais treize ans. J'ai participé à un concours pour trouver une actrice pour une publicité. J'ai gagné, et la publicité était un grand succès.

Puis j'ai enregistré une série qui traitait d'un élève au collège, que j'ai tournée pour la télé. C'est fini pour moi maintenant, mais c'est bien. Je suis trop âgée pour ce rôle, et on cherche un remplacement.

Je vais apparaître dans un film au mois de novembre qui traite d'une famille qui se perd dans la montagne. Ce film aura lieu dans les Alpes, près du Mont-Blanc, et aussi en Suisse.

On loge dans un petit hôtel près de Grenoble, mais aussi lorsqu'on tournera le film, on logera dans un refuge dans la montagne, très haut dans la montagne, et à 15 kilomètres du prochain village. Je l'attends avec impatience.

Après ça, je vais arrêter de tourner des films pendant un an, pour pouvoirme concentrer sur mes études pour mon baccalauréat. Puis j'aimerais aller en fac, peut-être aux États-Unis, avant de continuer de participer au monde du cinéma et de la télévision, que j'adore.

1 **when she was thirteen**
2 **she is too old for the role now**
3 It is about a family who **are lost in the mountains.**
   The film will take place in **the Alps (or near Mont-Blanc).**
4 **in a small hotel; near Grenoble; also in the mountains; in a refuge/ hut; 15 kilometres from the nearest village** (any three)
5 **in the USA/America**

Learning

Je suis au Collège Desmoulins depuis quatre ans, et je suis en troisième maintenant. Notre collège commence le matin à huit heures et demie, et termine à cinq heures de l'après-midi. L'après-midi, l'école commence à deux heures, donc je peux rentrer chez nous à midi.

C'est beaucoup plus long que la journée chez vous, et puis normalement j'ai des devoirs pour une heure et demie chaque soir. Là, il n'y a personne pour m'aider, alors je dois résoudre mes problèmes moi-même, ou bien envoyer des questions par texto ou email à mes copains.

En général j'aime bien mon école, car j'ai des profs sympas, et puis je suis fort en sciences et maths, donc les examens dans ces matières, ça va. Le jeudi matin, j'ai chimie, que je trouve très intéressante, et puis les sciences naturelles que je trouve passionnantes! Ma prof d'anglais, elle s'appelle Mme Albert. Elle nous donne beaucoup de devoirs. Je la trouve assez sévère, bien qu'elle nous aide quand nous avons des problèmes.

Ce vendredi, c'est le dernier jour avant les vacances: après nous avons les vacances de Pâques. Nous avons des vacances bien plus longues que chez vous!

1 **he goes home for lunch**
2 I do homework for **an hour and a half every night.**
  I have no one to help me, so **I solve my problems myself /
  sometimes I text or mail my friends about the homework.**
  (either one)
3 **he has nice/good teachers; he is good at science and maths; he
  finds the exams straightforward** (any two)
4 **she gives lots of homework; she is strict; she helps with problems**
  (any one)
5 His day **is much longer than in Scotland.**
  The holidays **are much longer in France.**

Employability

Je n'ai pas aimé l'école, parce que les journées étaient très longues, surtout parce que j'avais un trajet de quarante minutes en car chaque jour, et des devoirs pendant deux heures chaque soir.

Je vais aller en fac à Nice. Je veux assister à des cours en langues vivantes, et l'Université de Nice est connue pour l'anglais et l'italien. En plus, la ville de Nice offre beaucoup d'activités culturelles!

Je vais loger chez mon copain Eric, qui est à Nice depuis un an déjà. Il a un appartement dans un immeuble au centre-ville. C'est cher, mais il m'est important de vivre en centre-ville.

Cet été je vais travailler chez mon oncle pour gagner de l'argent pour l'université. Il tient une ferme dans le sud-ouest de la France, et je vais assister à la vendange. Je travaillerai pendant six semaines.

Quand je serai à Nice, je sais que je devrai trouver un petit boulot pour pouvoir payer le loyer de mon appartement. J'ai déjà travaillé comme serveur dans un restaurant, et je vais chercher un poste comme ça.

1 **the days were very long; he had a 40-minute bus journey every
  day; he had two hours' homework a night** (any two)
2 The University of Nice **has a good reputation for languages / English
  and Italian.** (either one)
  Moreover, the town of Nice **has lots of cultural activities (there is
  lots to do).**
3 **with his friend (Eric); in a flat; in the centre of town** (any two)
4 This summer he will **work for his uncle / work on a farm** (help with
  the grape picking) **in south-west France.** (either one)
  In Nice he will look for a job to **pay for his rent / his apartment.**
  (either one)

Culture

Je suis allée en Amérique du Sud, car mon père est espagnol et je parle la langue, et aussi car je voulais faire un très long voyage, un voyage qui m'emmenerait loin de chez moi.

Je suis allée en Patagonie, au sud de l'Argentine. Ce n'était pas très loin de l'Antarctique.

J'ai passé le premier mois chez une famille argentine, dans leur ferme. Après, j'ai voyagé dans le vrai sud, et j'ai été dans une tente pour la plupart du temps; quelquefois je me suis installée dans une pension pour une nuit.

Je supportais très mal la température. Il faisait très froid, et il y avait toujours un vent très fort. Un jour le vent a pris ma tente, et toutes mes affaires ont été mouillées par la pluie.

Ce qui m'a le plus impressionnée, c'était la solitude, et le fait que tout le monde était beaucoup moins stressé et en hâte que chez nous. La vie était lente. Je me suis changée, dès mon voyage.

1 **her father is Spanish; she speaks the language; she wanted to go on a long journey** (any two)
2 **Patagonia** or **South Argentina**
3 She spent the first month **with a family on their farm.**
   When she was in the real south, mostly she **was in a tent / camping.**
4

| She did not mind the cold temperature. | F |
| Once all her things got soaked by the rain. | T |

5 Overall she liked the journey because **of the solitude / people were less stressed / hurried.** (any one)

Dialogues

Society

Amélie: *Alors tu as vu que* Nouvelle Star *est de retour? Pour moi, c'était toujours la meilleure des émissions de téléréalité. La* Nouvelle Star, *ça fait deux ans que c'est fini et il est grand temps qu'elle revienne.*

Christophe: *Pour moi la téléréalité, c'est la télé que je déteste. Ce n'est pas du tout la réalité, tout est organisé et prévu à l'avance.*

Amélie: *Ce n'est pas vrai! Tu sais qu'il y a 25 000 personnes qui participent aux sélections, qui viennent de partout en France et Belgique.*

Christophe: *Mais pour la plupart, ils n'ont pas de chance de réussir.*

Amélie: *Alors oui, je trouve ça horrible comme on montre à la télé les gens qui ne peuvent pas chanter, les 'inoubliables', pour qu'on puisse rire sur ces pauvres. Comment doivent-ils se sentir quand ils se voient à la télé et que tout le monde les trouve amusant?*

Christophe: *Alors tu es d'accord avec moi!*

Amélie: *Mais voilà Christophe Willem par exemple, qui connaît un succès phénoménal et a reçu à chaque émission la majorité des votes du public.*

Christophe: *Il en y a très peu qui réussissent comme ça. Pour la plupart, on ne connaît plus leurs noms aujourd'hui.*

Amélie: *Alors, de toute façon, moi je vais être prête à donner un coup de téléphone pour voter ce week-end!*

Christophe: *Moi je ne vote que par texto: c'est beaucoup moins cher!*

1 For her it was **the best reality show on TV.**
   It has not been on **for 2 years.**
   It is **high time it was back.**

2 **there are lots of participants (25,000); from all over France and Belgium**

3

It is horrible the way they show people who cannot sing.	T
People laugh at them.	T
The singers find it amusing seeing themselves on TV.	F

4 Christophe Willem, for example, **was very (phenomenally) successful.**
   Every show he **won the majority of votes.**

5 **Amélie will phone vote; Christophe will vote by text**

Learning

Adrienne: *Alors Richard, ça fait deux ans que tu es en école à Édimbourg. Comment tu le trouves?*

Richard: *Eh bien, c'est très différent de mon ancien collège. Tout va beaucoup plus vite: ça commence à neuf heures, on court de classe en classe, la récré et la pause déjeuner sont vite finies (une heure au total!), mais je suis chez moi à quatre heures chaque jour!*

Adrienne: *Vraiment? Chaque jour?*

Richard: *Alors non, pas exactement, parce que le mardi j'ai entraînement de rugby (je suis membre de l'équipe de rugby de l'école), et quelquefois le mercredi on a un jeu après l'école.*

Adrienne: *L'école a sa propre équipe?*

Richard: *Oui, c'est normal en Écosse. L'école a toute sorte d'équipes et de clubs: le hockey, le basketball, les échecs, les débats, bon, beaucoup. Ce sont les profs de l'école qui organisent tout ça.*

Adrienne: *Chez moi il n'y a rien comme ça, mais je ne sais pas si je l'aimerais. Je préfère voir mes profs en classe, puis c'est fini!*

Richard: *Non, ça marche, car ils semblent différents quand ils ne sont plus dans la salle de classe. On peut leur parler et discuter avec eux.*

Adrienne: *Et les devoirs, comment ils sont?*

Richard: *Bien voilà une différence que j'apprécie beaucoup ici. En France, j'aurais sûrement des devoirs pour une heure et demie chaque soir, tandis qu'en Écosse je peux souvent finir mes devoirs en trente minutes. Pour mes devoirs de français il me faut deux minutes.*

Adrienne: *Ah, ça c'est le paradis!*

Richard: *Oui, dans un certain sens, mais remarque que nous n'avons que six semaines de vacances l'été, et deux jours en février.*

Adrienne: *Quoi? Alors moi, je ne déménage jamais en Écosse. Pour moi, les deux semaines de vacances d'hiver et les neuf semaines en été, je ne les abandonnerais jamais!*

1 **everything goes much faster; it starts at nine; he only has an hour for break and lunch; he is home by 4p.m** (any three)
2 It is **normal in Scotland.**
   The school has **lots of teams and clubs.**
   It is organised by **teachers from the school.**
3 **the teachers are different outside class; you can talk to them/ discuss or argue with them** (either one)
4 **in France he would have an hour and a half every day; in Scotland he is finished in 30 minutes**
5 **he only has 6 weeks' holiday in the summer; and 2 days for the February holiday**

Employability

Marc: *Eh bien, comment as-tu trouvé ton stage en entreprise?*

Hélène: *C'était bien, j'ai aimé les gens avec lesquels je travaillais, et le magasin était intéressant pour moi, car ils vendaient des articles de sport et comme tu sais, moi je suis sportive!*

Marc: *Comment as-tu fait au début?*

Hélène: *J'ai pris contact avec le propriétaire de l'entreprise et après, je suis allée me présenter et rencontrer mon tuteur, qui travaillait dans le magasin et s'occupait de moi pendant que je faisais mon stage.*

Marc: *Comment as-tu préparé ton stage?*

Hélène: *Je me suis informée des conditions de travail dans l'entreprise, les horaires de travail, les vêtements que je devais porter, etc.*

Marc: *Et à la fin, comment ça a marché?*

Hélène: *J'ai parlé avec mon tuteur et avec le propriétaire à la fin. J'ai discuté de mes réussites et les difficultés que j'ai rencontrées. Et maintenant, je reste en contact avec mon tuteur. J'ai écrit une lettre de remerciements, et je le tiens informé des résultats de mes examens. Il va m'aider avec ma recherche d'emploi l'année prochaine.*

1 **she liked the people she worked with; she found the shop interesting; she is very into sport and it was a sports shop**
2 She made contact with **the owner of the shop.**
   After that she **went to meet her tutor (supervisor).**
   Her tutor **worked in the shop/looked after her.** (either one)
3 **working conditions; working hours; clothes she should wear** (any two)
4 **she met with her tutor and the owner; she discussed her successes and the difficulties she met** (either one)

5	She discussed her placement with her tutor and her boss.	T
	She has written a thank you letter to her tutor.	T
	He will help her with her exams.	F

Culture

Caroline: Tu sais, cet été je vais aller en Italie pour passer trois semaines chez une famille italienne.

Daniel: Mais pourquoi tu fais ça?

Caroline: Alors, j'ai commencé l'italien au collège, et tu sais comme j'aime bien être le meilleur dans la classe. Et puis, je veux bien voyager indépendamment, sans mes parents pour la première fois.

Daniel: Tu apprends aussi l'anglais. Pourquoi ne pas aller en Angleterre?

Caroline: J'ai déjà visité l'Écosse avec mes parents. Nous y sommes allés il y a deux ans. Et puis, je suis très forte en anglais. Donc, l'Italie c'est plus important en ce moment. Et en plus, il va faire plus beau là!

Daniel: Ah, c'est ça! Tu cherches le soleil et tu veux bronzer!

Caroline: Non, non. La famille habite à Rome, et ce n'est pas le cas que je vais bronzer. Je vais connaître une culture nouvelle, manger des choses différentes, voir les grands monuments, tout ça!

Daniel: Eh bien, moi je préfère rester en France. J'aime la cuisine et la culture française. Si je veux manger des plats italiens, je peux commander une pizza.

1 **going to Italy; for 3 weeks; staying with an Italian family**
2 She has started **learning Italian (at school)**.
She always likes to be **best in the class**.
She would like to travel **independently/without her family for the first time**.

3	She wanted to visit Scotland.	
	She was there 2 years ago.	T
	She does not like English.	
	Italy is more important for her right now.	T
	The weather will be better there.	T

4 **getting to know a new culture; eating different things; seeing the sights (monuments)**

Chapter 8

Talking: Preparing for the assessment

Introduction

Talking is worth 30 marks, or 25 per cent of your overall mark, and it is a key skill. You will have to carry out a talking assessment as part of your exam. The topic for this assessment will be agreed by you and your teacher, and your performance will also be marked by your teacher. It will be recorded, and may well be sent off to SQA for moderation. This is a part of the course you can do very well in, if you get the preparation right. And remember, this is a performance. The subject you choose will probably be from one of the four contexts: **society**, **learning**, **employability** or **culture**. You will find a more detailed list on page viii in the introduction.

The rules are quite clear: there will be two parts to the assessment, which will take place at the same time. The first part will be a presentation on a subject of your choice. The second part will be a 'natural, spontaneous' conversation, starting with the area you have talked about in your presentation. The presentation will be worth 10 marks and the conversation will be worth 20 marks. Of those 20 marks, 5 marks will be available for making the conversation sound natural, not just reciting things you have learned by heart! We will look at this later. The whole assessment should last at least 6 or 7 minutes. You will be allowed to have a certain number of words as notes to help you through your presentation, as well as visual aids. (This could be objects, pictures or a PowerPoint presentation, for example.) You will be allowed up to five headings with eight words in each heading. Your talk will be graded according to the categories in the marking instructions on pages 60–61. Look carefully at the categories, and decide which grade you are going to aim for. If you are looking for an A, for instance, then you will be expected to put in a variety of structures, such as some conjunctions and sub-clauses.

You will know the topic for the formal assessment beforehand so you can prepare for it. This is a huge advantage.

In this chapter we will look at the two parts of the task in detail, and give you advice and support on preparing for what you will have to do.

The presentation

For this, you will have to talk on a subject of your choice for about one and a half minutes. You should prepare this presentation well in advance, and learn it so that you can be absolutely sure of what you have to do.

You must be reasonably accurate in your use of French, and use tenses well. The grammar guide in Chapter 11 shows what examiners are going to be looking for. Your vocabulary should be at the right level and should give you a chance to show many of the things you have learned about the topic you are presenting. Your presentation should have a good structure. You also need to make sure what you say sounds like French, that is, the way a French person might sound. That means you should work on your pronunciation!

Planning your presentation

When you have a subject for your assessment, try to break it down into three or more sections and prepare each one separately. This will make it easier to remember and will give you a structure. You are allowed some headings as support. This is handy, as if you are nervous and get a bit mixed up in one part, you can recover in the next part with the help of your key words. You can have up to five headings of eight words each.

Once you have chosen your topic area, focus on the actual language you will use. Here are a few dos and don'ts.

Hints & tips ⭐

Dos

✓ Do look at the textbook or texts you are working from for good ideas you can use.

✓ Do make sure you understand what you are saying, or it will be very difficult to remember it properly.

✓ Do show a draft to your teacher to get suggestions or make corrections if necessary.

✓ Do use a variety of structures; avoid starting every sentence with **je**, for example.

✓ Do vary your tenses, and put in some joining words like **parce que** or **quand**.

✓ Do give your opinion, and work at having different ways of saying what you think. Look at the 'Giving opinions' section in Chapter 11.

✓ Do try recording your talk and listening to it to check your pronunciation.

Don'ts

✓ Don't leave the preparation to the last minute! If you start your preparation early, you will be able to ask your teacher for advice on any vocabulary or grammar you are unsure of.

✓ Don't always stick to safe, simple language. It may be easier, but won't get the best grades. Try out some of the more impressive sentences you have learned. Note down useful vocabulary and phrases you have seen elsewhere on this or other topics so you can reuse them in your talking assessment.

✓ Don't use lists of things (such as school subjects, places in town or favourite foods) to try to make your talk longer as this will count against you.

To help you prepare for a presentation, we have selected four possible topics (one each from **society**, **learning**, **employability** and **culture**) and will guide you through the process involved in preparing for and carrying out the assessment. You can follow the same pattern for a topic of your own choice. You might also find Chapter 9 'Writing': The final exam useful when preparing for a specific talking task.

Possible topics:
- Society: Healthy eating!
- Learning: Comparing education systems – an exchange visit
- Employability: Discussing work experience
- Culture: Discussing a film you have watched

Society: Healthy eating!

This topic will allow you to talk in the third person, use lots of opinion words and use good phrases from the texts you are working from. Your first task should be to look at your source texts to get ideas for your presentation. Then break your task into areas. You could start with a section in which you talk about what young people in Scotland actually eat, then talk about the dangers of fast food and bad eating habits, and finish off with what you think people should do. If you have some material on what people eat in France, you could use this as well as or instead of the ideas above. For the follow-up conversation, be prepared to talk about *your* eating habits, likes and dislikes, as well as anything you might know about food in France.

The first section might sound something like this.

Chez nous on mange beaucoup de bonbons, de fast-food, et il semble que les Écossais aiment manger des frites avec chaque repas. Beaucoup de jeunes ne prennent pas de petit déjeuner et arrivent au collège avec un Mars et une canette de coca. On ne mange pas beaucoup de fruits et de légumes, et l'idée de cinq portions par jour ne semble pas réussir chez nous.

The second section is where you put in your longer sentences, while explaining what the dangers are.

Il est malsain de sortir le matin sans petit déjeuner, car sans nourriture on ne peut pas bien travailler à l'école: on ne peut pas se concentrer et apprendre. C'est aussi dangereux de manger trop de graisse parce que la mauvaise nourriture peut encourager les maladies. Quand on ne mange pas assez de fruits et de légumes, il y a aussi des problèmes avec les dents, donc il faut aller plus souvent chez le dentiste.

In the final section you have the chance to show off all your ways of expressing opinions and making demands.

Il faut changer ce que les jeunes Écossais mangent. Nous ne devons pas accepter que les marchands de fast-food et de malbouffe vendent leurs produits dans nos cantines. Je trouve indéfendable que cette possibilité existe. On doit défendre aux écoles d'avoir des distributeurs de boissons gazeuses et de barres de chocolat. Nous devons encourager les jeunes à penser à leur avenir et à adopter de bonnes habitudes à l'école.

Learning: Comparing education systems – an exchange visit

You decide to do your presentation on an exchange visit, which will compare the school you visited with your own. Sort out your ideas and choose the areas to fit the topic. You will then find it easier to prepare each area in more detail. You might start with how you got to the exchange school, move on to a description of the school day in your own and the exchange school, and then describe the facilities in the two schools. Finally, you could talk about which aspects you find better or worse in each school. This topic is good for the follow-up conversation, as you will be able to prepare lots of questions and answers on schools.

Look at the vocabulary and language you have in your textbooks and material you have from school, and take what you think might help you. Look also at the suggested structures and vocabulary in Chapters 11 and 12 and take a few you think will fit in with what you are going to say.

Once you have chosen the kinds of thing you are going to say, think about the first section. You might decide to talk about how you got to your partner school. This will allow you to use the past tense to describe your journey. You can fit in time and place words and phrases. You will be able to use the vocabulary you know for methods of transport and give your opinions on these. You can also introduce a couple of good structures to show you know lots of good French! Here is an example of the kind of thing you can say.

> *L'année dernière je suis allé chez mon correspondant, qui habite en France. Je suis parti avec mon école et notre prof de français nous a accompagnés. Le voyage était très long, car on a pris le bus de Glasgow à Douvres, puis le ferry de Douvres à Calais. En France, le voyage a duré six heures! Quel long voyage! Mais le voyage était quand même super, parce que j'étais avec mes amis, et on a écouté de la musique et regardé des vidéos dans le bus!*

This would take about half a minute to say and would be an easy introduction. Once you have produced the first part, choose the key words that you will use as headings to help you when you carry out your presentation. They could be the first few words of your talk to get you started, or key words from throughout the different sections, or a phrase that you always find hard to remember exactly. What is important is that they help you remember your talk better.

The second section of your presentation could be about the school your pen pal goes to and its daily routine. This paragraph can be in the present tense, and allows you to compare a French school to your own school and to give opinions. Look at the phrases at the top of the following page and try to put together your own paragraph. Make sure you put in some opinions and comparisons, although most of these will be in the final paragraph.

Il y a une bibliothèque et une cantine.	*There is a library and dinner hall.*
Chez eux, on a le droit de …	*They are allowed to …*
Chez nous, on a le droit de …	*We are allowed to …*
On n'a pas le droit de …	*We/they are not allowed to …*
Il y a … élèves et … professeurs.	*There are … students and … teachers.*
On n'a pas besoin de porter l'uniforme scolaire.	*You don't have to wear school uniform.*
Le collège commence à … et finit à …	*School starts at … and finishes at …*
C'est un grand bâtiment moderne.	*It is a large modern building.*
C'est un collège mixte.	*It is a mixed school.* (both boys and girls)

When you are preparing your paragraph, remember not to produce a list of things the school has, and try to vary the language. Include some opinions and comparisons. Here is an example of what you could say.

Le collège de mon correspondant, qui s'appelle le Collège Victor Hugo, est un petit bâtiment gris au centre-ville. Il n'est pas très moderne. Chez eux, il y a une petite cantine, qui est beaucoup plus petite que chez nous. Il y a 600 élèves et 49 profs dans le collège; les cours commencent à 8h30 tous les jours et finissent à 16h30, ou quelquefois à 17h30. Quelle longue journée! Il n'y a pas d'uniforme scolaire chez eux, et je trouve bizarre de voir tous les élèves en jean et baskets.

Finally, you could prepare a section on your impressions of the school, comparing it to your own. This last section is also very much in the present tense, but in the sample answer we have finished off with a different tense, the conditional, and also put in a couple of future tenses. It also allows us to use the third person, varying our structures. And remember, keep putting in opinions as well as comparisons.

Mon correspondant aime son école, mais je trouve la nôtre beaucoup mieux. Nous avons beaucoup plus de possibilités pour le sport, et les salles de classe sont très mal équipées chez eux. Ce qui est bien chez lui, c'est qu'on a deux heures pour le déjeuner. En plus, si un prof est absent, on peut faire ses devoirs ou rentrer à la maison. Parce que c'est un collège, mon correspondant va devoir quitter son école cet été pour aller au lycée dans la ville d'à côté. Moi, je serai dans la même école que maintenant, mais en seconde. Je ne voudrais pas changer d'école l'année prochaine.

Employability: Discussing work experience

In this, you decide to talk about work experience that you undertook. As a topic, it allows you to use lots of past tenses, give opinions and then move on to talk about your future plans. It is also good for the follow-up conversation, as there will be many opportunities for you to prepare answers to the kind of questions you will be asked.

Decide on your structure first. The first paragraph could be about where you worked and what you did there. The second one could describe your daily routine and what you thought of different aspects of your work. Finally, you could move on to talk about how you liked your work experience, what it has taught you and what it will mean for your future.

In the first paragraph, you could say when the work experience took place and give details of where you worked, the hours you worked and how you got there. It is easy to start off this way as it is straightforward to remember. It could go something like this.

> *En octobre, j'ai participé à un stage en entreprise. J'ai travaillé pendant une semaine chez un coiffeur. Pendant cette semaine, toute la classe n'était plus à l'école, super! J'ai dû commencer à neuf heures du matin, mais le coiffeur était tout près de chez moi, donc je pouvais rester encore trente minutes au lit. Je suis allé au travail à pied.*

For the second paragraph, describe your daily routine, remembering to give some opinions about what you did.

> *Je n'ai pas pu couper les cheveux, mais j'ai appris à laver les cheveux des gens, sans leur mettre du shampooing dans les yeux! Je devais aussi balayer le plancher toutes les dix minutes, offrir des magazines aux clients et bien sûr préparer du thé ou du café pour tout le monde assez souvent. Tout le monde boit beaucoup de café là-bas! J'ai fini le travail à quatre heures et demie tous les jours, un peu plus tard que l'école, mais je n'ai pas trouvé ça un problème. J'ai reçu trois pourboires, ce qui était fantastique!*

For the third paragraph you could talk about how you liked the experience, what was good or bad and what you have learned from it. Here are some ideas.

> *J'ai bien aimé mon travail, et ils m'ont offert un job tous les samedis, un job que j'ai encore. C'est bien, parce que beaucoup de mes copines n'ont pas de travail. J'ai appris qu'on doit toujours sourire pour les clients, et je sais parler des vacances avec tout le monde! Je ne crois pas que je vais devenir coiffeuse, parce que je veux faire des études à l'université, mais si je n'ai pas de bonnes notes en Highers, je vais peut-être changer d'avis.*

Culture: Discussing a film you have watched

It is always a good idea when learning French to watch some films in French. It helps with your ear for French and improves your listening and talking. French films are easy to come by on DVD or online, and you can watch them with either French or English subtitles. You could ask your teacher for recommendations.

If you do watch a film, then it makes a great topic for a talking assessment, as you can retell the story, give your opinions on the film and compare it to some English language films you have seen. You could look on the internet to see what French people thought of the film – visit www.amazon.fr to read some reviews (*commentaires*).

As an example, let's look at *Être et Avoir*, which is a film set in a small primary school in central France where all the pupils are in one class. Your first paragraph could tell the story of the film.

Dans une petite école primaire en Auvergne, nous voyons une année dans la vie des élèves. Il n'y a que treize élèves dans l'école, avec un seul professeur, M. Lopez. Nous suivons les enfants au cours de l'année, surtout Jojo, et nous les voyons rire et pleurer, travailler et jouer.

In the second paragraph, you can say which bits you liked, or indeed what you didn't like! This gives you the chance to use opinion phrases.

Le film est très lent, et ce n'est pas très passionnant, mais c'est une histoire très simple et j'ai compris beaucoup du français qu'ils parlent. J'ai aimé voir les petits enfants visiter le collège de la ville voisine en fin d'année, et j'ai aussi aimé voir comment ils font leurs devoirs à la maison. Le professeur était super, très gentil, très patient et les enfants étaient très naturels. À la fin, j'avais l'impression de savoir comment ça marche, une école primaire en France.

Finally, you can compare what you saw with what you know yourself. This allows you to bring in some past tenses and to compare your own culture with that in France.

Mon école primaire était très différente. Il y avait 450 élèves et nous étions 30 dans ma classe. Mais une bonne partie du film ressemblait à mes expériences. Je n'ai jamais vu un film à la télé qui montre une école comme ça en Écosse. Chez nous, nous voyons les problèmes ou nous regardons des programmes à la télé comme Waterloo Road. *J'ai beaucoup appris en regardant ce film!*

The conversation

Once you have delivered your presentation, your teacher will engage you in a conversation about what you have said. This should last about 5 minutes. You should prepare for this as thoroughly as you can. And remember, you should carry out the conversation using *vous*, not *tu*.

Preparing for the conversation is not really very different from preparing for the presentation. You know what topic area you are going to discuss, and you can have your answers ready for this. You will not need to remember a big piece of text, but you will have to recognise which question needs which answer. You can also ask your own questions, and you should be ready to deal with the unexpected. This is not as difficult as it sounds, as there is a set of things you can do that will help you.

You could earn another five marks for making your conversation 'natural'. You can find the criteria for this on page 61. What does this mean? Firstly, make sure you ask questions as well as answer them. Secondly, do not just blurt out your answers. Take your time! Have ready the kind of little filler words and phrases that people use when they need time to think. For example, '*Eh bien*', '*Un moment, laissez-moi réfléchir*', '*Alors, vous savez*'. Look for more phrases to add to this list. Thirdly, do not be frightened to ask for repetition or clarification: '*Pouvez-vous répéter la question, s'il vous plaît?*' '*Pardon, je n'ai pas compris.*'

The first thing you need to know are the question words, so you understand what is being asked of you. Here are the main ones you will meet.

Qui *or* Qui est-ce que	*Who*
Qu'est-ce que *or* Qu'est-ce qui	*What*
Quand *or* Quand est-ce que	*When*
Où *or* Où est-ce que	*Where*
Quel *or* Quelle	*Which*
Pourquoi *or* Pourquoi est-ce que	*Why*
Comment *or* Comment est-ce que	*How*
Combien	*How much* or *How many*

Remember that in English we use 'do' to make a question: 'do you have', 'do you know' and so on. In French, questions are normally made with *est-ce que*: *est-ce que tu as, est-ce que tu sais* and so on. Let us look at making up questions. There are three main ways to do this.

1 Start with a question word if you need one. Add *est-ce que*. Then carry on with subject and verb as in a normal sentence.
2 Another way to ask a question is just to change the way you say a sentence, by making your voice rise at the end.
3 The third method is inversion, that is, changing the order of the subject and the object: *Avez-vous*?

Let us look at the topic, *Healthy eating!*, which was used on page 53 to demonstrate a presentation. Below is a list of possible questions you might be faced with in a conversation on this topic. The list includes different ways of asking questions, but that will not affect your answers. Try to write your own answers to the questions, using the vocabulary you know from studying this topic and remembering to refer to pages 74–75, where you will find guidelines on giving your opinion. Then have a look at the sample answers on the following page. Remember this is a conversation, so you should be ready to ask some of these questions yourself. You can either just ask them, or, if you have just been asked one, after your answer you can say *Et vous*? and then repeat the question.

Est-ce que votre santé est importante pour vous?	
Pourquoi?	
Comment est-ce que vous trouvez les repas à la cantine du collège?	
Votre famille aime manger sain?	
Comment trouvez-vous les plats végétariens?	
Qu'est-ce que vous faites pour garder la forme?	
Qu'est-ce que vous mangez au petit déjeuner normalement?	
Qu'est-ce que vous buvez avec votre repas à midi?	
Combien de bonbons est-ce que vous achetez chaque semaine?	
Qu'est-ce que vous avez mangé/bu à midi?	

Est-ce que votre santé est importante pour vous?	Oui, elle est très importante pour moi.
Pourquoi? (what you will be asked if you just say oui to the previous question)	Parce que je n'aime pas être malade, et je suis aussi très sportif/sportive.
Comment est-ce que vous trouvez les repas à la cantine du collège? (whatever your answer, try to say at least two things)	Je les trouve affreux. Je n'aime pas du tout manger à la cantine.
Votre famille aime manger sain? (again, two things at least; you could include yourself in the answer as well)	Mes parents aiment manger sain, mais mes sœurs préfèrent les hamburgers.
Comment trouvez-vous les plats végétariens? (allows you to use a different tense)	Je n'aimerais pas devenir végétarien, parce que j'aime trop la viande.
Qu'est-ce que vous faites pour garder ta forme? (a chance to say lots here)	Je fais du sport trois fois par semaine, je mange bien et je me couche tôt.
Qu'est-ce que vous mangez au petit déjeuner normalement? (again, say lots, but don't use lists)	Normalement, je prends des céréales avec du lait, et un fruit.
Qu'est-ce que vous buvez avec votre repas à midi? (use this opportunity to put in an opinion)	Je ne bois jamais de coca. Je préfère boire de l'eau ou du thé.
Combien de bonbons est-ce que vous achetez chaque semaine? (allows you to use a past tense)	Je n'achète plus de bonbons: j'y ai renoncé il y a six mois.
Qu'est-ce que vous avez mangé/bu à midi? (again, a chance to say a lot here but avoid lists)	J'ai mangé un sandwich et un fruit en centre-ville avec mes copains.

Remember

☞ Use the material you have researched for your presentation to give you a series of possible answers to questions. Put them down as a list of bullet points for revision.

☞ As it is a conversation, prepare a good half dozen questions you can ask your teacher (interlocutor!). So, if your presentation is on schools, ask your teacher what they think about your school and your partner school, what they think about the differences between the systems, what they like or dislike about their job. If you are discussing a film, ask your teacher if they have seen it, what their opinion of it was, what they liked best and so on.

☞ Practise using **vous** when in conversation. When you are talking to an adult and you use their surname rather than their first name, you need to use **vous**. Try this out in class with other students, so you get in the habit of using the correct word.

☞ Be prepared to answer questions that ask for your opinions.

☞ Be ready to lead the conversation into other areas if you feel you have run out of things to say. Your teacher will follow if you do this.

☞ Try to include some words or phrases to make it feel like a 'natural conversation'.

Your presentation and conversation will be marked according to the following criteria:

Presentation			
Content	Accuracy	Language resource	Pegged Marks
The candidate: • uses content which is relevant and well-organised • expresses a wide range of ideas and opinions • speaks without undue hesitation	The candidate: • demonstrates a very good degree of grammatical accuracy corresponding to the level, although may make a few errors which do not detract from the overall impression • uses pronunciation and intonation which are sufficient to be readily understood by a speaker of the language	The candidate: • uses **detailed** language throughout • uses a wide range of structures • uses a wide range of verbs/verb forms, tenses (if appropriate) and other language features	10
The candidate: • uses content which is mostly relevant and well-organised • expresses a range of ideas and opinions • may speak with occasional hesitation but recovers successfully	The candidate: • demonstrates a good degree of grammatical accuracy corresponding to the level. Errors may occasionally detract from the overall impression • uses pronunciation and intonation which are sufficient to be understood by a speaker of the language	The candidate: • mostly uses **detailed** language • uses a range of structures • uses a range of verbs/verb forms, tenses (if appropriate) and other language features	8
The candidate: • uses content which is generally relevant and well-organised • expresses some ideas and opinions • hesitates on a few occasions, but attempts to recover	The candidate: • demonstrates an adequate degree of grammatical accuracy corresponding to the level, although errors detract from the overall impression • uses pronunciation and intonation which are sufficient to be understood by a speaker of the language, although some points may not be immediately clear	The candidate: • attempts to use **detailed** language • attempts to use a range of structures • uses a few different verbs/verb forms, tenses (if appropriate) and other language features	6

Conversation			
Content	Accuracy	Language resource	Pegged Marks
The candidate: • uses content which is relevant and • well-organised • expresses a wide range of • ideas and opinions • covers a different context to that used in the presentation	The candidate: • demonstrates a very good degree of grammatical accuracy corresponding to the level, although may make a few errors which do not detract from the overall impression • uses pronunciation and intonation which are sufficient to be readily understood by a speaker of the language	The candidate: • responds using a wide range of **detailed** language • responds using a wide range of structures • responds using a wide range of verbs/verb forms, tenses (if appropriate) and other language features	15

⇨

Conversation			
Content	Accuracy	Language resource	Pegged Marks
The candidate: • uses content which is mostly relevant and well-organised • expresses a range of ideas and opinions • covers a different context to that used in the presentation	The candidate: • demonstrates a good degree of grammatical accuracy corresponding to the level. Errors may occasionally detract from the overall impression • uses pronunciation and intonation which are sufficient to be understood by a speaker of the language	The candidate: • responds using a range of **detailed** language • responds using a range of structures • responds using a range of verbs/verb forms, tenses (if appropriate) and other language features	12
The candidate: • uses content which is generally relevant and well-organised • expresses some ideas and opinions • may not cover a different context to that used in the presentation	The candidate: • demonstrates an adequate degree of grammatical accuracy corresponding to the level, although errors detract from the overall impression • uses pronunciation and intonation which are sufficient to be understood by a speaker of the language, although some points may not be immediately clear	The candidate: • attempts to respond using **detailed** language • attempts to respond using a range of structures • responds using a few different verbs/verb forms, tenses (if appropriate) and other language features	9

Conversation — natural element	
The candidate readily sustains the conversation, for example:	Pegged Mark
• understands almost all of what is said • speaks without undue hesitation or recovers successfully when there is such hesitation • deals with unpredictable elements • may occasionally seek clarification in the modern language • may take the initiative (e.g. ask relevant questions and/or expand on an answer) • may use some interjections and/or connectives	5
The candidate adequately sustains the conversation, for example:	Pegged Mark
• understands most of what is said • hesitates occasionally, affecting the flow of the conversation • mostly deals with unpredictable elements • may attempt to seek clarification in the modern language, but not always successfully • may occasionally take the initiative • may attempt to use some interjections and/or connectives, but not always successfully • may require some support and/or prompting from the interlocutor	3
The candidate has difficulty in sustaining the conversation, for example:	Pegged Mark
• understands only some of what is said • hesitates in most responses • has difficulty dealing with most unpredictable elements • requires support and/or prompting from the interlocutor • may attempt to seek clarification in the modern language, but often unsuccessfully	1
The candidate cannot sustain the conversation, for example:	Pegged Mark
• understands little of what is said • is unable to seek clarification in the modern language or does so ineffectively • hesitates throughout • is unable to deal with unpredictable elements • requires significant support and/or prompting from the interlocutor	

Introduction

The final writing exam is worth 20 marks or 12.5 per cent of your overall mark. You have to produce one piece of writing in the National 5 French external exam. The writing paper is given to you at the same time as the reading paper, and you have 1 hour 30 minutes in which to do both. That means you should reckon on about 30 minutes to plan, write and proofread your piece. This is very possible, as much of what you will have to write is predictable, and you can plan for this in advance.

The task will be based on a scenario given in English, along with a job advert in French. You will be required to provide specified information in a piece of writing of 120–200 words. You will be able to use a dictionary while doing the exam. The scenario always involves you writing to apply for a job or a work experience placement, in the form of an email.

The scenario is always given with six bullet points that you have to cover. The first four bullet points are the same every time; the last two will change a bit from year to year.

You can use textbooks and work you have already produced to guide you in your preparation. You can also work from guidelines provided by your teacher. This means you can really plan out a lot of what you want to write before the day of the exam.

Your writing will be graded according to how well it demonstrates a sense of structure and control of grammar, and how it addresses the bullet points. The mark categories for Writing show you how the examiners will judge how well you have done. These are included at the end of the chapter and show you what is expected of you. You will get a grade based on the quality of your writing, and then you may have marks subtracted from the total for each bullet point you miss out. This means it is important you do not miss out any bullet points, and you address each one in your writing. Tick them off on your exam paper as you go to make sure you have covered every single one, and indeed *each part* of them. Look at Chapter 11 'Structures and opinions' to see the kind of language that will gain you the best marks.

Preparing for writing

Let us look at an example of a writing paper. After this, we will look at the kind of general basic answers you should be prepared to write. This should help you write an essay based on this question. When you have done that, ask your teacher (very nicely, of course!) to mark it.

You are preparing an application for the job advertised below and you write an email in French to the company.

> **Café Georges** au centre de Bruxelles cherche serveur/serveuse.
>
> Vous devez être motivé et dynamique et savoir parler le français et l'anglais.
>
> Pour plus de détails ou si ce poste vous intéresse contactez Mme Georges à l'adresse suivante cafegeorges@fsnet.fr.com.

To help you to write your email, you have been given the following checklist of information to give about yourself.

You must include all of these points:
- *personal details (name, age, where you live)*
- *school/college/education experience until now*
- *skills/interests you have that make you right for the job*
- *related work experience*
- *when you will be available for interview and to work*
- *your experience of working with the public.*

Use all of the above to help you write the email in French. The email should be approximately 120–200 words. You may use a French dictionary.

You will see that there are six bullet points you have to cover, as well as bearing in mind the instructions at the top. This means you cannot simply prepare a piece of writing, learn it, then write it out again in the exam. The first four bullet points are very predictable, but the last two will be unique to that exam, so you will have to be ready to be flexible. You have to write 120–200 words in total, so a good rule of thumb is that each bullet point should have at least twenty words, with one or two being a bit longer. If your writing is not evenly balanced, you might lose points; however, it makes sense to have 100–120 words to cover the first four points, leaving you less to write in the two bullet points which are unpredictable. This guideline also makes it easier to keep track of how much you are writing, rather than always recounting words and wasting time.

What will you find easiest to prepare? Here is a list of things that should come up in the first four bullet points.
- personal details (name, age, where you live)
- school/college/education experience up to now
- skills/interests you have that make you right for the job
- any related work experience.

For the first point, use straightforward writing you know will be correct. This will give a good first impression. For instance:

> *Bonjour! Je voudrais me présenter. Je m'appelle Sean Wright. J'habite à Glasgow en Écosse. J'ai seize ans, et je suis né le 16 juin 20... (25 words)*

It is helpful to identify clearly your surname, as it might not be obvious to a French reader which this is, as they sometimes write their family name first.

The second bullet point is again straightforward, but remember you will be penalised if you simply give a list of subjects. For example:

> *Je suis à présent élève à Deadwood High, où je suis en seconde. J'ai eu de bonnes notes dans mes classes, et je suis particulièrement fort en sciences. J'apprends le français depuis cinq ans.* (34 words)

There are lots of other things you could say instead, but remember if you are writing to someone in France, they will not know what your qualifications are. And do not try to put too much in here. The key point is accuracy, plus some variety of language and structures. You could also change it so it is in the past. For example:

> *J'étais élève à Deadwood High, jusqu'au 30 juin. J'ai eu de bonnes notes dans mes classes, et j'étais particulièrement fort en sciences. J'ai appris le français pendant cinq ans.* (29 words)

For the third bullet point, your skills and interests should be appropriate to the job or placement you are applying for, so you might have to make some slight adjustments. However, most of this can be quite general. Here is an example:

> *Je m'entends bien avec tout le monde, et je comprends le français quand on le parle, parce que j'ai passé beaucoup de temps chez une famille française. Je m'intéresse beaucoup aux ordinateurs et aux nouvelles technologies.* (36 words)

Think about your own strengths. You should have a variety prepared, so you can check that the strengths you write down in the exam fit with the post in the question. But remember, for a top mark you need to include some conjunctions in your writing.

The fourth bullet point refers to related work experience. You could, of course, say you have never done any work experience, but it will be easier to make something up. 'Related' is something you can do easily. If you have done work experience in a shop or a hairdresser's (even just stacking shelves), you can say you are used to working with customers. If you have been in an office, you have experience in using computers and working with others. The relationship is between the work experience you have described and the post you are looking for. Here are two ideas:

> *J'ai déjà travaillé dans un grand supermarché pendant deux ans, donc je sais bien travailler avec les clients. J'ai un bon contact avec les clients, on m'a dit.* (28 words)

> *J'ai travaillé dans le bureau de mon oncle pendant trois mois cette année, donc je sais bien travailler avec les autres et aussi me servir des téléphones et des ordinateurs, surtout les programmes Microsoft.* (34 words)

The last two bullet points in the task ask when you will be available for interview and to work and about your experience of working with the public.

The last two bullet points in this writing task are meant to be unpredictable, and they will vary depending on what kind of job you are being asked to apply for. So you do need to have thought a bit about what might be asked of you, and you also need to have looked carefully at the job on offer, to guide you in your answers. However, the questions will all be related to applying for a job! Other possibilities of what could be asked in the last two bullets include:

- your strengths
- your experience of travelling to other countries
- whether you have already been to France
- what you do in your free time
- what sports you are interested in
- which languages you speak
- why you are interested in the job
- your experience of working generally
- to ask questions relating to the job.

If you have written a reasonable amount for the first four bullet points, then you need to write about fifteen words for each of the last two points, so think of one or two sentences at most. Ideally, you would have most of the possible questions covered by having tried them in advance.

Let us go back to the job at Café Georges and look at the second-last bullet point: when you will be available for interview and to work. The easiest way to answer this is to say 'I can be in Brussels on 1 June for an interview, and I can start work on 2 June.'

> *Je peux être à Bruxelles le premier juin pour un entretien, et je peux commencer le travail le 2 juin.* (20 words)

To get top marks you could say *Je pourrais* instead of *je peux*, and add in *si cela vous convient* ('if that suits you'). This allows you to use modal verbs with an infinitive.

The final bullet point is: your experience of working with the public. This is something you should have ready, whether you have had a part-time job or not! If you have not had a job, invent one. You could say something like 'I work on Saturdays in the supermarket in my town. I serve our customers all day'.

> *Le samedi, je travaille dans un supermarché à Glasgow. Je sers nos clients toute la journée.* (16 words)

To get top marks you could add *Je m'entends très bien avec mes clients*, or add in an opinion (something positive!) about your work, or put it in the past, to show you can use a variety of tenses – *j'ai travaillé, j'ai servi, je me suis très bien entendu* (*entendue* if you are a girl!).

Now look at the other possibilities in the bullet points above, and try to write 15–20 words for each. Ask your teacher to check what you have written.

So, hopefully you can see that the writing exam is not just a leap in the dark. You will be able to prepare most of the bullet points in advance, as long as you are able to be flexible. Now try to write an answer to the Café Georges sample question, and show your work to your teacher.

What you should do next is look at the writing task in other languages or in past or practice exam papers, which you can find on the SQA website. You could buy the papers or ask your teacher to share them with you. Look at the first four bullet points in each of them, then the last two, and see how much of each of these papers you can prepare in advance. You should look at the unexpected material, and plan how you would answer the last two bullet points.

The mark categories for writing are as follows:

Category	Mark	Content	Accuracy	Language resource – variety, range, structures
Very good	20	The job advert has been addressed in a full and balanced way. The candidate uses detailed language. The candidate addresses the advert completely and competently, **including information in response to both unpredictable bullet points**. A range of verbs/verb forms, tenses and constructions is used. Overall this comes over as a competent, well thought-out and serious application for the job.	The candidate handles all aspects of grammar and spelling accurately, although the language may contain one or two minor errors. Where the candidate attempts to use language more appropriate to Higher, a slightly higher number of inaccuracies need not detract from the overall very good impression.	The candidate is comfortable with the first person of the verb and generally uses a different verb in each sentence. Some modal verbs and infinitives may be used. There is good use of adjectives, adverbs and prepositional phrases and, where appropriate, word order. There may be a range of tenses. The candidate uses co-ordinating conjunctions and/or subordinate clauses where appropriate. The language of the email flows well.
Good	16	The job advert has been addressed competently. There is less evidence of detailed language. The candidate uses a reasonable range of verbs/verb forms. Overall, the candidate has produced a genuine, reasonably accurate attempt at applying for the specific job, even though he/she **may not address one of the unpredictable bullet points**.	The candidate handles a range of verbs fairly accurately. There are some errors in spelling, adjective endings and, where relevant, case endings. Use of accents is less secure, where appropriate. Where the candidate is attempting to use more complex vocabulary and structures, these may be less successful, although basic structures are used accurately. There may be one or two examples of inaccurate dictionary use, especially in the unpredictable bullet points.	There may be repetition of verbs. There may be examples of listing, in particular when referring to school/college experience, without further amplification. There may be one or two examples of a co-ordinating conjunction, but most sentences are simple sentences. The candidate keeps to more basic vocabulary, particularly in response to either or both unpredictable bullet points.
Satisfactory	12	The job advert has been addressed fairly competently. The candidate makes limited use of detailed language. The language is fairly repetitive and uses a limited range of verbs and fixed phrases, e.g. *I like, I go, I play*. The candidate copes fairly well with areas of personal details, education, skills, interests and work experience but does not deal fully with the two unpredictable bullet points **and indeed may not address either or both of the unpredictable bullet points**. On balance, however, the candidate has produced a satisfactory job application in the specific language.	The verbs are generally correct, but may be repetitive. There are quite a few errors in other parts of speech – gender of nouns, cases, singular/plural confusion, for instance. Prepositions may be missing, e.g. *I go the town*. Overall, there is more correct than incorrect.	The candidate copes with the first and third person of a few verbs, where appropriate. A limited range of verbs is used. Sentences are basic and mainly brief. There is minimal use of adjectives, probably mainly after *is*, e.g. *Chemistry is interesting*. The candidate has a weak knowledge of plurals. There may be several spelling errors e.g. reversal of vowel combinations.

Category	Mark	Content	Accuracy	Language resource – variety, range, structures
Unsatisfactory	8	The job advert has been addressed in an uneven manner and/or with insufficient use of detailed language. The language is repetitive, e.g. *I like, I go, I play* may feature several times. There may be little difference between Satisfactory and Unsatisfactory. **Either or both of the unpredictable bullet points may not have been addressed.** There may be one sentence which is not intelligible to a sympathetic native speaker.	Ability to form tenses is inconsistent. There are errors in many other parts of speech – gender of nouns, cases, singular/plural confusion, for instance. Several errors are serious, perhaps showing mother tongue interference. The detail in the unpredictable bullet points may be very weak. Overall, there is more incorrect than correct.	The candidate copes mainly only with the personal language required in bullet points 1 and 2. The verbs *is* and *study* may also be used correctly. Sentences are basic. An English word may appear in the writing. There may be an example of serious dictionary misuse.
Poor	4	The candidate has had considerable difficulty in addressing the job advert. There is little evidence of the use of detailed language. Three or four sentences may not be understood by a sympathetic native speaker. **Either or both of the unpredictable bullet points may not have been addressed.**	Many of the verbs are incorrect. There are many errors in other parts of speech – personal pronouns, gender of nouns, cases, singular/plural confusion, for instance. The language is probably inaccurate throughout the writing.	The candidate cannot cope with more than one or two basic verbs. The candidate displays almost no knowledge of the present tense of verbs. Verbs used more than once may be written differently on each occasion. Sentences are very short. The candidate has a very limited vocabulary. Several English words may appear in the writing. There are examples of serious dictionary misuse
Very poor	0	The candidate is unable to address the job advert. The two unpredictable bullet points may not have been addressed. Very little is intelligible to a sympathetic native speaker.	Virtually nothing is correct.	The candidate may only cope with the verbs *to have* and *to be*. Very few words are written correctly in the modern language. English words are used. There may be several examples of mother tongue interference. There may be several examples of dictionary misuse.

Introduction

During the course of your studies, you will have to carry out a writing assignment. This writing is worth 20 marks, or 12.5 per cent of your overall National 5 result. The assignment will be marked externally by SQA. The subject of this piece of writing will be set by your teacher in discussion with you: your teacher might suggest a choice of topics to write about or you may suggest a context/topic of your own. You can decide together what format the task set will be in: bullet points, questions or statements. Whatever format you choose, the actual task will be set by your teacher in English, not in French. The subject or topic for this piece of writing must be taken from one of the contexts of **society**, **learning** or **culture**.

Once you know what the topic is, you can use textbooks and work you have already produced to guide you in your preparation for tackling the assignment, and this means you can really plan what you hope to write. You should plan to write 120–200 words.

You will be presented with the questions or bullet points, or a choice of several tasks, on the day you actually write the assignment. The assignment must be written in class under controlled conditions, with only a dictionary, verb or grammar guide and your memory to help you! You will not be allowed any notes or rough drafts to work from. The kind of documents you could have with you are given below.

- grammar reference notes (including verb tables)
- a bilingual dictionary
- a word or vocabulary list
- the writing stimulus presented to you on the day of the exam (bullet points or equivalent in English).

When you have finished, you will hand your work over to your teacher. They will look at it and decide whether it is good enough to send off to SQA, or whether they treat it as a first draft, give you some suggestions as to how to improve it and ask you to try again, under the same controlled conditions. This can, however, only happen once, so your second attempt will be the final one. If you do have a second draft, you will also be allowed two additional items given below.

- a writing improvement code (if your teacher has used this to annotate your first draft, in order to see how to improve your work)
- the first draft of your writing annotated by your teacher, whether in a writing code or comments at the end.

The rules for the assignment are very open: you can write in a whole variety of different styles and there is no type of writing you *must* use. The only specification is the writing should be of a factual nature. When you are handed the list of bullet points, statements or questions you can choose which ones to address: you do not have to answer them all and you could also introduce other material you think relevant to the task. You might find that the topic you are using for your writing assignment will also work later for the presentation or discussion in your talking assessment, which could save you time and effort.

Your writing will be graded according to how well it demonstrates a sense of structure, control of grammar, focus on the task and communication. The exact criteria consist of the ability to:

- use detailed written French language
- use language accurately to convey meaning
- express ideas and opinions and use content relevant to the task
- 'demonstrate language resource'–that means showing you can use French correctly–and employ a range of vocabulary, structures and, where appropriate, tenses.

You should try to use a variety of tenses and structures. You should be able to give your opinions on what you are writing about, both positive and negative, if possible. Your writing should always focus on the topic you have chosen, so what you write should be relevant to your chosen title.

For a mark of 16 or 20, you will have to use more complex and sophisticated language. You must be reasonably accurate in your use of French and use tenses well. Your opinions will be important, and you should try to include reasons for some of these opinions. Your writing will have to be varied and flexible!

The way of judging how well you have done is given in the marking instructions for writing and shown below. This table will let you see what is expected of you for a mark of 12, 16 or 20.

Content	Accuracy	Language resource	Pegged marks
The candidate: - addresses the title in a full and balanced way - uses content which is relevant - expresses a wide range of ideas, opinions and reasons - writes in a very structured and organised way and the language flows well	The candidate: - demonstrates a very good degree of grammatical accuracy corresponding to the level, although may make a few errors which do not detract from the overall impression - demonstrates a very good degree of accuracy in spelling and, where appropriate, word order	The candidate: - uses **detailed** language throughout - uses a wide range of structures - uses a wide range of verbs/verb forms, tenses (if appropriate) and other language features	20
The candidate: - addresses the title competently - uses content which is mostly relevant - expresses a range of ideas, opinions and reasons - writes in a structured and organised way	The candidate: - demonstrates a good degree of grammatical accuracy corresponding to the level; errors may occasionally detract from the overall impression - demonstrates a good degree of accuracy in spelling and, where appropriate, word order	The candidate: - mostly uses **detailed** language - uses a range of structures - uses a range of verbs/verb forms, tenses (if appropriate) and other language features - may occasionally repeat structures, verbs, etc.	16

Content	Accuracy	Language resource	Pegged marks
The candidate: • addresses the title fairly competently • uses content which is generally relevant • expresses some ideas, opinions and reasons • writes with an adequate sense of structure and writing is mostly organised	The candidate: • demonstrates an adequate degree of grammatical accuracy corresponding to the level, although errors, which occasionally may be serious, detract from the overall impression • demonstrates an adequate degree of accuracy in spelling and, where appropriate, word order • produces more correct language than incorrect	The candidate: • attempts to use detailed language • attempts to use a range of structures • uses a few different verbs/verb forms, tenses (if appropriate) and other language features • may use fairly repetitive language • may use some lists	12

Planning your writing

Once you have chosen your topic area, focus on the actual language you will use. Try to look at three to five headings to break the task down for you. Preparing a writing assignment is very like preparing a talk, so you might also find it useful to look at Chapter 8 'Talking: Preparing for the assessment'. The do's and don'ts are very similar for both.

Hints & Tips ★

✓ Do look at the textbook or texts you are working from for good ideas you can use.

✓ Do make sure you understand what you are writing, or it will be very difficult to remember it properly when you have to do the final writing for the assignment.

✓ Do use a variety of structures: use different tenses, joining words (parce que, quand) to make longer sentences, adjectives, adverbs and phrases you know are correct.

✓ Do write in paragraphs to give your writing a sense of structure: try to address each bullet point, question or statement in a new paragraph.

✓ Do think about an introduction and a conclusion to help the sense of structure.

✓ Do give your opinion and work at having different ways of saying what you think. Look at Chapter 11 'Structures and opinions' for support with this.

✓ Don't leave the preparation to the last minute! If you start your preparation early, you will be able to ask your teacher for advice on any vocabulary or grammar you are unsure of.

⇨

> ⇨
> ✓ Don't always stick to safe, simple language. It may be easier, but it will not achieve the top grades. Note down useful vocabulary and phrases you have seen elsewhere under appropriate topic headings so you can reuse them in your writing assignment. Try some of the more impressive sentences you have come across and kept for this purpose.
> ✓ Don't use lists of things as these will not help you to show structure or knowledge of French. What will be more important than the actual number of words is the range and variety of structures. So, 120 words could be absolutely enough; you do not have to pad out the writing to achieve a better grade.

Start to collate a number of sentences on the topic you can use: many of them should involve using sub-clauses and you should think about ways of introducing different tenses.

When you are ready, decide on a title (in French) for your piece of writing and make sure you know which of the three contexts (**society**, **learning** or **culture**) the topic relates to.

Finally, on the day of the assignment, remember you are only allowed the items listed on page 68 and your memory. You should not be using your dictionary at this stage to look up any new words, as this might introduce fresh errors! Instead, use it as you go along and after you have finished to check what you have written for accuracy. Remember also to look at your verb endings, as the accuracy of these will have a big influence on the grade you are awarded. Use the verb pages in your dictionary to check your endings!

You do not have a set time to produce the writing and you could tackle it over more than one period, as long as you hand in the material you are working on to your teacher before you leave the class. Once you have completed a draft, your teacher might annotate it and let you see this before you attempt the final draft. However, you cannot take it home to work on: it has to stay in class.

SQA have published a number of possible scenarios for the writing assignment. Below is one such example in detail.

French (Culture): Tourism in my region/area

An online tourist forum requests contributions for opinions on Scotland. The forum asks members living in Scotland to write about their own town/area.

Write 120–200 words in French. You could include:

● where your town/region is situated
● what it is like, why you like it/good points and bad points
● the weather
● areas or sites of interest for visitors/tourists
● any tourist information and useful advice for coming to Scotland.

For this topic, you do not have to address all the bullet points, so choose the ones you have good material for. If you address four bullet points, it means about 30 words for each one, and if you address three, it means 40 or so words for each. And remember, you should be expressing opinions, so the second bullet point is a good one to go for! You could also include a past tense, saying what you used to find good or bad.

J'aime bien ma ville, parce qu'il y a beaucoup à faire et à voir, mais ce que je n'aime pas, c'est que … Quand j'étais plus jeune, j'aimais beaucoup …, mais maintenant cela ne m'intéresse plus.

The final bullet points are also a chance to use future and conditional tenses, as well as the command form of the verb. They also enable you to include weather aspects and cover that point at the same time.

Je recommanderais une visite à … Il y aura une fête le 10 juillet à … N'oubliez pas d'apporter une parapluie, car il pleut quelquefois en Écosse.

Think about a short introduction, and a conclusion.

Aujourd'hui, je voudrais parler un peu de Perth, la ville où j'habite.

Alors, maintenant vous savez un peu de ma région : j'espère que vous l'avez trouvé intéressant.

The important thing, is not to try and write something in English, then translate it into French. It is much better to collect sentences from your French resources and put them together. If you are lucky, in the local tourist office you might find brochures in French about where you live which could be of support here. Otherwise, try using a search engine and put in the name of where you live along with *français* and see what comes up.

When you have enough material together, try to write 120 words and see what that looks like. If you think it is good enough, ask your teacher if you can try to write out an assignment. This will be good practice for the task itself, particularly if your teacher is using a correction code, as you can see how that works in practice. Below is an example code that could be used: this one is complicated, so if your teacher uses one like this, you need plenty of practice in applying it.

Code	Meaning
^	omission/something missing
aa	adjectival agreement/problem with agreement of the adjective(s)
acc	accent missing
ap	adjectival position/problem with position of adjective(s)
dict	dictionary/wrong word
ew	extra word/words not required
g	gender
gr	grammar problem/incorrect grammar
mv	missing verb
mw	missing word

Code	Meaning
np	new paragraph
ns	new sentence
prep	preposition to check
punct	punctuation
rep	repetition
s? (text underlined)	not making sense
sg/pl	singular/plural
sp	spelling
struct	structure — incorrect or does not exist
t	tense
ve	verb ending
vt	wrong verb tense
wo	word order
ww	wrong word

If you are attempting the formal writing assignment for the first time, try to follow the steps below.

- Look carefully at the task set, whether it is bullet points, questions or statements.
- Decide which ones you are going to address.
- Start with a brief introduction.
- Write a paragraph of 30–40 words for each bullet point, making sure each paragraph has at least one sub-clause and finding places to use a variety of tenses.
- Finish with a brief conclusion.
- Use your dictionary or word list only to check the spelling of words you have written, not to look up new terms: you can do this as you write, but it is also part of the final proofreading process.
- Use your verb tables to check the endings of the verbs you have used.

If you have been handed back your assignment with either comments or a correction code, take your time to look carefully at the comments or signs. If there is something you do not understand, you can ask your teacher to explain what it means. When redrafting, remember you will have a copy of the code used with you, as well as your first draft. When you are ready, you should carefully rewrite your assignment, changing it in accordance with your teacher's suggestions. Take care not to add new errors when copying your work: take your time, and check regularly as you go through the process to make sure you have copied the relevant material accurately. You can highlight bits of the original once you have copied them, to make sure you have everything included! Use your dictionary to check spelling and accents, particularly if these have been commented on. Use your verb tables where your endings or tenses may be incorrect in order to find the correct version. Only hand your work in when you are sure it is correct!

Chapter 11

Structures and opinions

To help you in both talking and writing, this chapter should act as a reference when producing your own work. As you may see when you look at the mark categories for writing on pages 66–67 and 69–70, and for talking on pages 60–61, you will be assessed in both writing and talking on your use of structure, your use of opinions and reasons, your use of a variety of grammatical structures and tenses, as well as of, course, the accuracy of your talking and writing. You should try to make sure that your preparation for talking and writing works towards these mark categories.

Structure

This means that your work should be directly related to the topic you are talking or writing about, and should also hang together. You should not just collect a whole set of different phrases and sentences, and jumble them all together. For talking, best of all is the structure where you introduce the topic, give your opinions and then come to a conclusion. You should avoid the temptation to give long lists; when talking about sport, for instance, do not simply give a list of sports you do, and when talking about television, avoid a list of your favourite programmes. Avoid starting every sentence the same way, as in *Je* ... For writing, you will be asked to produce a piece of writing answering six bullet points. The best solution is to use roughly the same number of words (25 or so) for each bullet point.

Giving opinions

You might find the following phrases useful when giving your opinions.

J'aime, J'adore, Je préfère	*I like, I love, I prefer*
Je n'aime pas, Je déteste	*I don't like, I hate*
J'ai horreur de ...	*I really hate ...*
Je trouve que c'est ...	*I think that it's ...*
Je trouve cela formidable	*I find that terrific*
Je trouve bête que ...	*I find it stupid that ...*
C'est fantastique, très bien, génial, intéressant, passionnant, marrant	*It's fantastic, very good, great, interesting, exciting, funny*

$\Rightarrow$

C'est minable, triste, déprimant, pénible, nul, ennuyeux	*It's awful, sad, depressing, difficult, no good, boring*
C'est mieux/pire de …	*It's better/worse to …*
Il y a (Il y avait) trop de …	*There is/are (There was/were) too much/many …*
Il n'y a pas assez de …	*There is not enough …*
Il serait utile de pouvoir …	*It would be useful to be able to …*
À mon avis …	*In my opinion …*
Il faut penser à …	*You have to think about …*
Il ne faut pas oublier que …	*We mustn't forget that …*
Nous devons … / Nous ne devons pas …	*We should … / We shouldn't …*
J'aimerais savoir que …	*I would like to know that …*
Je voudrais voir …	*I would like to see …*

Using conjunctions

Giving reasons for your opinions, or for why things happen, can be done by using conjunctions. This is a good idea, as it allows you to do two things at the same time: you are expressing yourself and you are also using more complex structures and language. Conjunctions, or joining words, are words like *car, parce que, donc, quand*, which say why something is the way it is. Look at the sentences below to see conjunctions in action when discussing how you get on with your family, giving an opinion followed by a reason. In your talking assessment, try to have at least two sentences like this in your presentation. Make sure you also include sentences like this in your preparation for the conversation.

Je n'ai jamais assez d'argent de poche, mais mes parents pensent que j'en ai assez.	*I never have enough pocket money, but my parents think I do.*
J'adore le vendredi, parce que tout le monde est content que c'est le week-end.	*I love Fridays, because everyone is happy it's the weekend.*
Mes parents n'ont pas beaucoup d'argent, donc il me faut travailler le samedi.	*My parents don't have a lot of money, so I have to work on Saturdays.*
J'aimerais que mes parents me donnent plus de liberté.	*I wish my parents would give me more freedom.*

Grammatical structures

The marks you get for your talking and writing assessments will be affected by the structures you use. Sometimes this means using good phrases and sentences you know, but often it is just a question of making sure all your sentences do not start with *je*. Make sure you create opportunities to use *nous* and *on* (remembering to get the verb ending right). Think about sentences in which you talk about what other people think or do. Here is a list of things you might consider putting into your preparation:

- attaching adjectives to nouns, with the correct endings
- using negatives with your verbs, putting the two words in the correct place
- using pronouns in your sentences
- using modal and impersonal verbs, such as *Je* **peux** *aller, On* **doit** *savoir que ..., Il* **faut** ...

The Language resource column in the mark categories table on pages 66–67 shows you what the examiner will be looking for.

Tenses

The final thing to think about is using a variety of tenses. Every talking or writing task should use at least two different tenses. This means planning the tenses in your preparation. If you are discussing your learning at school, for instance, you could say what things used to be like, what will happen next year, or what you would like to happen. If you are discussing mobile phones, again you can say what you or other people used to do, and what you intend to buy as your next model.

For the purpose of preparing for National 5 assessments, we can divide the tenses into three areas: present, past and future. Let us look at each of these three areas.

The present

The present tense only has one form, but you can expand on this by using modal or impersonal verbs. Here are some examples of this.

Je veux travailler le week-end.	*I want to work at the weekend.*
On ne peut pas prendre le train le samedi.	*You can't get the train on Saturdays.*
Il faut aller à Glasgow pour voir un film.	*You have to go to Glasgow to see a film.*
Je dois beaucoup aider à la maison.	*I have to help a lot at home.*

The past

You should be able to use two tenses in the past. These tenses have various names, although most books refer to them as the perfect and the imperfect tense. You should use the perfect tense to talk about an event in the past, and the imperfect tense to describe how things used to be. If your whole assessment is based on the past, then you should use both tenses. If most of what you are discussing is in the present, then put in one or both of these tenses as well. Here are some examples of the kind of thing you might say, when discussing your lifestyle and hobbies.

J'ai commencé de jouer au foot il y a quatre ans.	*I started to play football four years ago.*
Je jouais d'abord avec mes amis.	*I used to play with my friends at first.*
On a gagné la finale en 2013.	*We won the final in 2013.*
Je aimais beaucoup le foot.	*I used to like football a lot.*

The future

There are three different ways to talk about the future that you should be able to use. This is not as frightening as it sounds, as much of it is very straightforward. You should be able to demonstrate the use of the informal future tense, the formal future tense and the conditional tense. Below, you will find some examples of these, with sentences referring to your plans for the future.

The informal future is very easy: you just use the present tense of *aller*, together with the infinitive form of the verb you are using.

Je vais retourner à l'école l'année prochaine.	*I'm going back to school next year.*
On va aller en vacances ensemble.	*We're going to go on holiday together.*
Mes parents vont payer mes vacances.	*My parents are going to pay for my holiday.*

The formal future

This is the tense where you do have to know your endings, and where there are irregular verb forms, but you will find these in any good dictionary. Get into the habit of using your dictionary to check your verb endings.

J'irai à l'université.	*I will go to university.*
J'habiterai chez mes parents.	*I'll live with my parents.*
Ma copine ira à Aberdeen.	*My friend is going to go to Aberdeen.*

The conditional

This tense is very like the formal future in its formation, but has slightly different endings. There are, however, some very straightforward phrases using the conditional tense which would fit most pieces of writing. The conditional tense talks about what *could* happen. Here are four examples, used to talk about your plans for the summer.

J'aimerais aller en Espagne.	*I'd like to go to Spain.*
Je voudrais y aller avec mes amis.	*I'd like to go with my friends.*
Je ne travaillerais pas pendant les vacances.	*I wouldn't work during the holidays.*
Ça serait formidable!	*That would be great!*

Vocabulary

The vocabulary pages are here as a reference for you. You should check that you know the vocabulary in each area when getting ready for a listening or reading assessment, and use it as a revision guide. When you have a writing or a talking task, the vocabulary is here to help you with ideas. Starter sentences are given in some sections, but you should get into the habit of collecting your own sentences and phrases, things you know are right and you think will fit the task. Whenever you see a good phrase, just make a note of it in your notebook or vocabulary file.

These are the areas covered.

General vocabulary:
- Numbers, including times, dates, temperatures, distances and prices
- Days, months, weeks and years
- Weather

Society:
- Family
- Lifestyles
- Media
- Places in town

Learning:
- School subjects
- School – general vocabulary

Employability:
- Jobs and professions
- Work experience

Culture:
- Planning a trip
- Celebrating a special event
- Film and television

General vocabulary
Numbers
Times

neuf heures	nine o'clock
neuf heures et quart	quarter past nine
neuf heures vingt	twenty past nine
neuf heures et demie	half past nine
neuf heures moins le quart	quarter to nine
neuf heures moins cinq	five to nine
midi et demi, minuit et demi	half past midday/half past midnight
treize heures	1p.m.
dix-huit heures trente	6.30p.m.
le matin	morning
l'après-midi (m)	afternoon

Remember

Most official times in French will use the 24-hour clock, and there is no use of a.m. and p.m.

le soir	evening
la nuit	night

Days

lundi	Monday
mardi	Tuesday
mercredi	Wednesday
jeudi	Thursday
vendredi	Friday
samedi	Saturday
dimanche	Sunday

Months

janvier	January
février	February
mars	March
avril	April
mai	May
juin	June
juillet	July
août	August
septembre	September
octobre	October
novembre	November
décembre	December

Seasons

le printemps	spring
l'été (m)	summer
l'automne (m)	autumn
l'hiver (m)	winter

Dates and other time phrases

mercredi 25 novembre	Wednesday 25 November
Je suis né(e) le 14 octobre	I was born on 14 October
une semaine	a week
quinze jours	a fortnight
un mois	a month
un an	a year

J'ai quinze ans	I am 15
une année	a year (frequently used with an adjective)
une bonne année	a good year
mille neuf cent quatre-vingt-treize	1993

Weather

la météo	the weather forecast
Quel temps fait-il?	What is the weather like?
Il fait beau tous les jours	The weather is nice every day
Il y a de temps en temps du soleil	It is sunny now and then
Il fait chaud (Il ne fait jamais chaud)	It is hot (It is never hot)
La température est de 25 degrés	It is 25° centigrade
Il fait souvent mauvais	The weather is often bad
Il fait froid en hiver	It is cold in winter
Il gèle pendant la nuit	It freezes over at night
Il y a assez souvent du vent	It is quite often windy
Il y a du brouillard en automne	It is foggy in autumn
Il pleut maintenant	It is raining now
Il neige en hiver	It snows in winter
Il y a du vent	It is windy

Society
Family

la famille	family
les parents	parents
le père	father
la mère	mother
le mari	husband
la femme	wife
le frère, mon frère aîné/cadet	brother, my older/younger brother
la sœur, ma sœur aînée/cadette	sister, my older/younger sister
le fils	son
la fille	daughter
le grand-père	grandfather

Remember

☞ France, like most other countries in the world, uses centigrade to measure temperatures. So a weather forecast will say something like: **Aujourd'hui il va faire quinze degrés.** Make sure you know your numbers!

☞ You should never use measurements like miles when talking and writing in French, but always metres and kilometres: **Glasgow se trouve à 70 kilomètres d'Édimbourg. J'habite à 500 mètres de l'école.**

☞ Prices are all in euros and cents: **Un coca coûte 3 euros. J'ai payé 3,50 €.**

☞ When writing about yourself, you should use **livre** for pounds: **Je gagne 20 livres tous les samedis au magasin.**

la grand-mère	grandmother
le jumeau/la jumelle	twin
le petit-fils/la petite-fille/les petits-enfants	grandson/granddaughter/ grandchildren
la tante	aunt
le cousin/la cousine	cousin
le neveu	nephew
la nièce	niece
l'oncle (m)	uncle
Je fais du babysitting	I baby sit
Je fais la cuisine	I do the cooking/I cook
Je prépare le dîner	I make (the) dinner
Je fais du jardinage	I do (the) gardening
Je tonds le gazon	I cut the grass
Je fais mon lit	I make my bed
Je fais la vaisselle	I do the washing-up
Je fais la lessive	I do the washing
Je lave la voiture	I wash the car
Je mets la table	I set the table
Je débarrasse la table	I clear the table
Je passe l'aspirateur	I do the hoovering/I hoover
Je range ma chambre	I tidy my room
Je sors la poubelle	I take out the rubbish

Starter sentences

Souvent je dois faire les courses pour ma mère	I often have to do the shopping for my mother
De temps en temps, il me faut ranger ma chambre	Sometimes I have to tidy my room
Tous les jours, je fais mon lit – quelle barbe!	I make my bed every day – how boring!
Je ne fais jamais la lessive	I never do the washing
Nous sommes quatre dans ma famille	There are four of us in my family
Je n'ai pas de frères/sœurs	I don't have any brothers/sisters
Je suis enfant unique	I am an only child
J'ai une sœur et deux frères	I have a sister and two brothers
Mon frère/ma sœur s'appelle ...	My brother/sister is called ...

Mes parents s'appellent ...	My parents are called ...
Mes parents sont séparés/divorcés	My parents are separated/divorced
Je m'entends bien avec mes parents	I get on well with my parents
Je ne m'entends pas bien avec mon frère	I don't get on well with my brother
Mes parents sont très sympas	My parents are very nice
Ma sœur est très gentille	My sister is very nice
Quelquefois, je me dispute avec ma mère	Sometimes I argue with my mother
Je peux discuter de mes problèmes avec ...	I can speak about my problems with ...
Mon frère m'énerve	My brother gets on my nerves

Lifestyles

à peine	hardly
accro	addicted
l'activité physique (f)	physical activity
alcoolique	alcoholic (e.g. person)
alcoolisé	alcoholic (e.g. drink)
l'alcoolisme (m)	alcoholism
l'alimentation saine (f)	healthy diet
avertir	to warn/to inform
la crise cardiaque	heart attack
cru	raw
les crudités (f pl)	assorted raw vegetables
dégoûtant	disgusting
la dégustation	tasting (of food)
désintoxiquer	to detox/to treat for alcoholism or drug addiction
se détendre	to relax
la douleur	pain
s'entraîner	to train (e.g. in a sport)
épais	thick
épicé	spicy
épuiser	to exhaust
faire la grasse matinée	to have a lie-in

le foie	liver
gâcher	to spoil/to waste
hors d'haleine	out of breath
ivre	drunk
les matières grasses (f pl)	fat
mener	to lead
la piqûre	sting/bite
le poumon	lung
renoncer	to give up
reprendre connaissance	to regain consciousness
respirer	to breathe
salé	savoury/salty
sauvegarder	to save/to safeguard
savoureux	tasty
le sommeil (avoir sommeil)	sleep (to feel sleepy)
le tabagisme	addiction to smoking
le/la toxicomane	drug addict
tuer	to kill
la veine	vein

Media

chatter	to chat (online)
le clavier	keyboard
copier	to burn/to copy
l'écran (m)	screen
l'e-mail (m)/le courrier électronique	email
le forum	chatroom
l'imprimante (f)	printer
imprimer	to print
l'internet (m)	internet
le lien	connection, link
le logiciel	software
mettre en ligne	to upload
le mot de passe	password
numérique	digital
l'ordinateur (m)	computer

la page d'accueil	homepage
la page web	webpage
le programmeur	programmer
sauvegarder	to save, to store
le site internet/le site web	website
le hashtag	hashtag
le sondage	opinion poll/survey
la souris	mouse
taper	to type
télécharger	to download/to upload
la touche	key (of keyboard)
le virus	virus
la webcam	webcam

Places in town

l'aéroport (m)	airport
l'arrêt d'autobus (m)	bus stop
la banque	bank
le bâtiment	building
la bibliothèque	library
la boîte	(night) club
le camping	campsite
le centre commercial	shopping centre
le centre sportif	sports complex
le château	castle
le cinéma	cinema
la cité	housing estate
le collège/le lycée/ l'école (f)	lower secondary school/higher secondary school/primary school
le commissariat/la gendarmerie	police station
l'église (f)	church
la gare	train station
la gare routière	bus station
le grand magasin	department store
l'hôpital (m)	hospital
l'hôtel de ville (m)/la mairie	town hall

le magasin	shop
la maison des jeunes	youth club
le marché	market
le métro	underground
le monument	monument
le musée	museum
le parc	park
la patinoire	skating rink
la piscine	swimming pool
la place	square
le pont	bridge
le port	harbour, port
la poste	post office
le stade	stadium
la station-service	petrol station
le syndicat d'initiative/l'office (m) de tourisme	tourist information office
le théâtre	theatre
la zone piétonne	pedestrian precinct

Starter sentences

À Perth, il y a beaucoup à faire et à voir	There's lots to do and see in Perth
Il n'y a rien à faire pour les jeunes	There is nothing for young people
Chez nous, il y a une piscine	We have a swimming pool
Il n'y a pas de gare	There is no station
J'habite Dumfries depuis douze ans	I've lived in Dumfries for 12 years
Il n'y a pas grand-chose ici	There is not a lot here
Il n'y a pas de cinéma	There is no cinema
On peut aller à la maison des jeunes	You can go to the youth club
Je joue au foot tous les week-ends	I play football every weekend
Je vais au cinéma avec mes copains	I go to the cinema with my friends
Mon sport préféré, c'est le/la …	My favourite sport is …
Moi, j'adore jouer au tennis	I love playing tennis
Ce que je ne supporte pas, c'est …	What I really can't stand is …

Le mardi, je joue au hockey – c'est génial!	I play hockey on Tuesdays – it's brilliant!
Je suis membre d'un club de natation	I'm in a swimming club
Je suis membre de l'équipe de hockey	I'm in the hockey team

Learning

School subjects

l'allemand (m)	German
l'anglais (m)	English
les arts (m pl) plastiques	art, craft and design
la biologie	biology
la chimie	chemistry
le commerce	business management
le dessin	art
l'enseignement moral et civique (m)	citizenship
l'EPS (f)	PE
l'espagnol (m)	Spanish
le français ₎	French
la géographie	geography
l'histoire (f)	history
l'informatique (f)	IT
les maths (mpl)	maths
la musique	music
la politique	modern studies
la physique	physics
les sciences nat (f pl)	science/physics
la technologie	design and technology

School – general vocabulary

le bac/baccalauréat	equivalent to Highers
la bibliothèque	library
le bulletin	report
la cantine	canteen
le collège/CES	secondary school (S1–4)
le cours	lesson
les devoirs (m pl)	homework

l'école primaire (f)	primary school
un/une élève	pupil, student
les études (m pl)	study, schoolwork
l'examen (m)	exam
la fac/l'université (f)	uni/university
les grandes vacances (f pl)	summer holidays
le laboratoire	laboratory
les langues vivantes (f pl)	modern foreign languages
le lycée	secondary school (S5/6)
la maternelle	nursery school
la matière	subject
la pause de midi	lunchtime
le/la professeur/prof	teacher
la récréation/la récré	interval, break
redoubler	to retake a year at school
la retenue	detention
réussir	to pass/to succeed
la salle de classe	classroom
les vacances (f pl)	holidays
les vacances de Pâques, de Noël	Easter/Christmas holidays

Useful adjectives

bête	stupid
chouette	great/fun
difficile	difficult
dur	hard
ennuyeux	boring
facile	easy
faible (je suis faible en ...)	weak (I'm not so good at ...)
fort (je suis fort en ...)	strong (I'm good at ...)
intéressant	interesting
marrant	funny
nul (je suis nul en ...)	useless (I'm useless at ...)
passionnant	exciting, great
sévère	strict
utile	useful

Remember

☞ French secondary school classes are numbered backwards: they start in **sixième**, then go on to **cinquième**, **quatrième**, **troisième**, **seconde**, **première**, and, finally, **terminale**.

☞ When writing about school, do **not** give long lists of the subjects you take!

Starter sentences

Je vais passer mes examens en mai	I'm going to sit my exams in May
J'espère réussir mes examens	I hope to pass my exams
J'ai eu de bonnes notes en …	I got good marks in …
Ma matière préférée, c'est le français	My favourite subject is French
Ce que je n'aime pas du tout, c'est …	What I really don't like is …
Je pense que le prof est affreux	I think that the teacher is awful
Je trouve que j'ai trop de devoirs	I think I have too much homework
L'année prochaine, je vais continuer mes études au lycée	I'm staying on next year for Highers (NB this is the cultural equivalent and not direct translation)

Employability
Jobs and professions

acteur/actrice	actor
agent de police (policier/policière)	policeman/policewoman
agriculteur/agricultrice	farmer
avocat/avocate	lawyer
boucher/bouchère	butcher
boulanger/boulangère	baker
caissier/caissière	cashier
chauffeur de taxi	taxi driver
chômeur/chômeuse	jobseeker
coiffeur/coiffeuse	hairdresser
cuisinier/cuisinière	cook
dentiste	dentist
directeur/directrice	director
électricien/électricienne	electrician
facteur/factrice	postman/postwoman
steward/hôtesse de l'air	air steward
infirmier/infirmière	nurse
ingénieur/ingénieure	engineer (with a degree)
jardinier/jardinière	gardener
journaliste	journalist

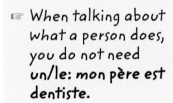

Remember

☞ When talking about what a person does, you do not need *un/le*: mon père est dentiste.

maçon	bricklayer
mécanicien/mécanicienne	mechanic
médecin	doctor
patron/patronne	boss
PDG	managing director
plombier/plombière	plumber
professeur	teacher
secrétaire	secretary
serveur/serveuse	waiter/waitress, barman
technicien/technicienne	technician
vendeur/vendeuse	shop/sales assistant

Starter sentences

Ma mère est professeur	My mother is a teacher
Je voudrais devenir infirmière	I would like to be a nurse
Je vais aller en fac	I'm going to go to university
Je veux continuer mes études	I want to stay on at school/ university
Le samedi, je travaille dans un café	I work in a café on Saturdays
J'ai un petit boulot comme vendeuse	I have a part-time job in a shop

Work experience

Pôle emploi	job centre
l'apprenti(e)/apprentissage	apprentice/apprenticeship
l'avenir (m)	future
le boulot	job
la carrière	career
le client/la cliente	customer/client
le commerçant	shopkeeper
construire	to build
économiser	to save
employer/employé(e)	to employ/employee
l'entreprise (f)	firm
l'entretien (m)	interview
les études (f pl) (à plein temps/à temps partiel)	full-time/part-time study
gagner	to earn, to win

s'inscrire	to enroll
le jour (de congé)	day (off)
le métier	trade/job
l'orientation professionnelle (f)	careers advice
l'ouvrier/ouvrière	worker/labourer
le paiement	payment
le patron	boss
poser sa candidature	to apply (for a job)
le poste	post, job
le progrès	progress
le projet	project
la salaire	salary/wages
le stage en entreprise	work experience/placement
la tâche	task
le travail	work, job

Culture
Planning a trip

amener, apporter	to bring
l'auberge de jeunesse (f)	youth hostel
avoir lieu	to take place
les bagages	luggage
se bronzer	to sunbathe
la côte	coast
défaire les bagages	to unpack
dresser/planter une tente	to put up a tent
l'endroit (m)	place
l'étranger/étrangère	foreigner
à l'étranger	abroad
faire les valises	to pack
la fiche	form
la frontière	border
l'île (f)	island
libre-service	self-service

le lieu	place
la location	hire/renting (out)
le logement	accommodation
loger	to stay
louer	to rent, to hire (out)
la mer	sea
le monde	world/people
le pays (natal)	(native) country
la plage	beach
quinze jours/la quinzaine	fortnight
se reposer	to have a rest
la réservation	booking
réserver	to book
rester	to stay/remain
le sac/sac à dos/sac à main	bag/rucksack/handbag
le sac de couchage	sleeping bag
le séjour	stay
semaine	week

Methods of transport

en auto/voiture	by car
en autobus/car	by bus/coach
en avion	by plane
en bateau	by boat
en métro	by underground
à moto	by motorbike
à pied	on foot
en train	by train
à vélo	by bike

Celebrating a special event

s'amuser	to have a good time/to have fun
un baiser, un bisou	a kiss (on the cheek)
le bal	dance
le boum/la fête	party
la bûche de Noël	Christmas log (a cake)
le cadeau	present

le colis	parcel
la distraction	leisure activity/something entertaining
l'exposition (f)	exhibition
les félicitations (f pl)	congratulations
fêter	to celebrate
les feux d'artifice (m pl)	fireworks
la foire	fair/show
l'invitation (f)	invitation
l'invité(e)	guest
inviter	to invite
le Jour de l'An	New Year's Day
le jour férié	bank or public holiday
les loisirs (m pl)	free time/leisure activities
le mariage	marriage, wedding
marié(e)	bridegroom (bride)
Noël	Christmas
Pâques	Easter
le parc/parc d'attractions	park/theme park

Film and television

acteur/actrice	actor/actress
animé	lively/animated
l'annonce (f)/la pub	announcement/advertisement
l'auteur	author
la bande dessinée (BD)	comic strip/book
la chaîne	channel/chain/music system
la chanson (populaire)	song
chanter	to sing
chanteur/chanteuse	singer
la chœur/la chorale	choir
comédien/comédienne	actor
un dessin/dessin animé	drawing/cartoon
dessinateur/dessinatrice	illustrator, draughtsman/ draughtswoman
distraire	to entertain/distract

le divertissement	entertainment
l'écran (m)	screen
l'émission (f)	programme
le feuilleton	serial/soap opera
le genre	sort/kind
il s'agit de	it's about
les informations/infos (f pl)	news
le journal	newspaper
les médias (m pl)	media
les nouvelles (f pl)	news
la pièce (de théâtre)	play
les prévisions météo (f pl)	weather forecast
la publicité, la pub	advertising, advert
le quotidien	daily paper
la revue/le magazine	magazine
le roman (policier)	(detective) novel
la séance	session/performance/showing
la série	series
sous-titré	sub-titled
le spectacle	show
les spectateurs (m pl)	audience
la télécommande	remote control
le télévision	television
le titre	title
la vedette	star

Space for extra vocabulary and notes on my answer in the writing

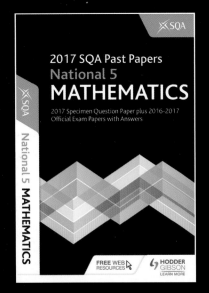
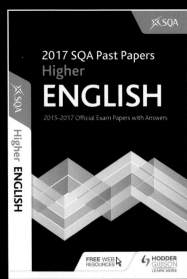
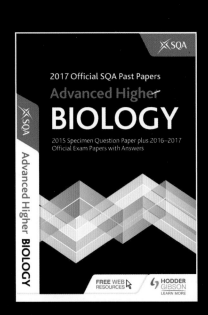